HOMELESS

David Brandon is the Senior Lecturer in Social Work at The Hatfield Polytechnic. He was born in 1941 and spent his childhood in Sunderland, County Durham where he first experienced homelessness. He holds a BA in Social Studies from Hull University and the Diploma in Mental Health from the London School of Economics. He has published many papers in such journals as *New Society* and *British Hospital Journal* and is the author of several pamphlets: *The Treadmill, Homeless in London, Women without Homes, The Decline and Fall of the Common Lodging House, Not Proven.* He is currently engaged on a Government sponsored research programme into the homelessness of young people.

HOMELESS

DAVID BRANDON

SHELDON PRESS
LONDON

First published in Great Britain in 1974
by Sheldon Press
Marylebone Road, London NW1 4DU

Printed offset in Great Britain by
The Camelot Press Ltd, Southampton

ISBN 0 85969 024 5 (cased)
ISBN 0 85969 025 3 (paper)

CONTENTS

ACKNOWLEDGEMENTS

My thanks to Nick Beacock (now Director of the Campaign for the Homeless and Rootless), Colin Hodgetts (Director of Christian Action), Richard Huson, Jennifer Clark and all the staff and residents at Greek Street, but especially to those six women who spent so much time telling me about their lives.

Chapters four, six and seven originally appeared in 'Women Without Homes', Christian Action Publications, 1971. My thanks to Christian Action for permission to reproduce those chapters here.

Where would I be without my loving Althea, Stewart and Toby?

INTRODUCTION

By now, homelessness has become my great obsession. Since I first encountered it as a teenager, it has dominated an ever-increasing portion of my life. My wife has made breakfasts for a wide assortment of unexpected visitors who have stayed a few nights at our home. I have given dozens of talks to women's institutes and rotary clubs; spoken often on radio and appeared on television. It has become a long love affair. Most of the hundreds of hours I have spent pounding the typewriter were devoted to writing about homelessness. On my bookshelves are hundreds of cuttings, books and pamphlets about housing and hostels, some now written by me.

Increasingly, I've spent long periods of time away from home. I've lost contact sometimes with my wife and two young children by spending nights on railway stations, talking to homeless men and women of all shapes and sizes, trying to understand the whys and wherefores of it. So well known has this obsession of mine become that many people, particularly in social work, link my name automatically with homeless single people.

But I understand much less about homelessness now than I did ten years ago. Time has blurred the major outlines and obscured the detail. I started in pursuit of simple answers to a series of questions and now I am left, not with answers, but with even more complicated questions. Much of the riddle lies within myself. Why does homelessness fascinate me so much? Why can't I leave it well alone and work with retarded children or the elderly? Part of the answer to that lies in the satisfaction of the love affair. I have put a lot into the field and received much more in return.

There is something very basic about people who have no home. All the great religious leaders have been restless wanderers. Homelessness is frequently not just the absence of roof, warmth and relationships but a state of mind. It is often the very bottom of poverty, the depth of despair. People with no roof have a sense of hopelessness, resignation and powerlessness.

Poverty does not of itself ennoble and there is little romantic within it. Sometimes however it does enable you to see people anew in a strong stark light which takes away all the trappings. I can discern elements of *King Lear* in the people amongst whom I work. When everything is taken away or more especially given up, some begin a journey, which can become an Odyssey, into themselves.

Some of the six women who appear later in this book have a shattering knowledge of themselves. They have been compelled, like tortoises, to carry absolutely everything important with them. They have been compelled to come to terms with fundamental and disturbing experiences which can both impoverish and uplift. The purposes of this book are to lay part of myself bare, to say something about the Greek Street community for homeless women, but most importantly to let six women have voices which may be heard and possibly have some small effect on the way we run our prisons and mental hospitals. I hope that soon we may not run them at all. If those six voices are heard clearly then this book will be worth while.

1

AN OBSESSION

My childhood in Sunderland was an unhappy one. My parents rowed continually. My father was an extremely unsuccessful and inefficient insurance agent in the colliery villages of Durham. In my early years he had periods of unemployment and we were very poor. Mother was a very hard-working seamstress whose noisy electric machine kept her children awake into the early hours of the morning. My own relations with my father were always stormy: he constantly nagged and bullied and often beat me. He tried to undermine everything that was important to me; sneering at my pacifism and Quaker beliefs, and making fun of my socialism. We quarrelled bitterly about the nuts and bolts of growing up: my staying out late at night, pocket money and relations with girl friends.

After one enormous row in which we came to blows, I ran away from home and tried to sleep on a hillside at Houghton Cut. It was bitterly cold and I had no warm clothing and could not sleep. Early in the morning it had begun to drizzle so I made my way back to town, defeated, and was picked up by the police. My father was furious and began to punch me almost before the policemen had departed. He seemed to have no desire to understand what had happened. My mother, the rock of our family, whom I so much admired, said very little but was obviously glad to see me come home. I cried myself to sleep and would have run away again the following morning but there was nowhere to go and no one who seemed to understand. I wanted to be left alone to grow up in my own way.

I became increasingly unhappy at home and a year

later I was shelterlessness in central London. This huge, strange city seemed very hostile to a sixteen year old Northerner. I had to speak very slowly and deliberately for my broad Durham vowels to be properly understood. I had no money and nowhere to go. On the advice of a police station I tried to get into the Salvation Army hostels but they were either full up or simply reluctant to interest themselves in a young lad with no money. As it got dark I became afraid and asked two city policemen for advice. They simply smiled blandly and told me that everywhere was full. I didn't even know where I was.

I spent the bitterly cold night on a large pile of news-papers under an arch in the Royal Exchange buildings in Threadneedle Street, in the very heart of the City of London. I was turfed off my temporary bed by an irate newspaper seller at around six o'clock on a cold rainy morning. I decided to go to Friends House, the national headquarters of the Quakers, to try and borrow money. I wandered around Euston Road for hours until the offices began to open. I was successful. They gave me money for my long rail journey and enough for food and drink. I went to King's Cross station for the first part of my repatriation. I drank large mugs of tea until the train came into the platform. It was beautiful to give the man my ticket and several hours later to arrive amongst the hills and slag heaps of my native Durham. My mother was glad to see me again.

It was several years before homelessness hit me again. I had just spent my first term at Hull University studying for a degree in social studies. I was beginning to read books about social problems rather than experience them directly. I was also slowly recovering from that cultural shock which entrance to University education with its totally different sets of values, frequently means for working class teenagers. Life at Hull was both intoxicating

and bewildering: a rapid round of parties, lectures and
seminars, eating in restaurants, learning to discuss a wide
range of subjects from physics to ballet with style and
panache but precious little knowledge. It was necessary
to change my eating habits, to bath more frequently, to
modify my accent, to discuss quietly and unemotionally
instead of with great waves of passion. I lived in a hall
of residence, in great contrast to my parents' cramped
council house in Sunderland. We dined off crested plates,
with silver cutlery on an oaken table. Radiators piped
heating all over the building whilst at home we had to
huddle over the open coal fire for comfort. There was a
hearty public school tradition among the 'chaps' which
could be suffocating. Home was a long way away, both
geographically and psychologically.

I knew that my parents' marriage was breaking up.
However it still came as a shock when I returned home
just before Christmas, 1960, to find that my younger
brother Eric and my mother had been dispossessed of
our council house and that my much disliked father was
living alone in considerable comfort. The floor of his
bedroom was covered with books and long playing
records. He smiled as I entered, sitting up in bed with
his cardigan pulled down over grubby pyjamas, surrounded by dirty plates and apple cores. I asked where
my mother and Eric were and was told that they had
gone to stay with my Uncle Louis.

I felt very angry. Uncle Louis was a retired bosun who
had run away to sea at fifteen. He was a thin wiry man
with a temper like a typhoon. He lived right across the
other side of the town in another small council house
on a vast estate. When I arrived my mother, who was
upset, told me that my father, who had not been living
at home for several months, had forced his way in one
night. He had been so obnoxious and so difficult to live

with that she had decided to retreat to her relatives. We spent a miserable Christmas living out the Christmas story. Meals were grabbed from a crowded table and I slept on two easy chairs in the tiny lounge while Eric snored his head off at my feet. Seven of us huddled in that three-bedroomed house. The people in that crowded house were my closest relatives but, at that time, I felt resentfully a thousand miles away from them. I did not stay very long. Over the New Year, after visiting housing offices and trying to explain the family's plight to blank administrative faces, I took to the road. I left the harassed family and hitch-hiked round the country to stay with several new college friends, whose parents had detached houses in Bristol and Leeds. When I came home, my father had disappeared with most of the furniture and we were able to return to the house, albeit empty. My mother had worked so hard to furnish it, to make the curtains and lay the carpets and now, out of sheer spite, my father had taken it all away. It could be of no possible use to him. But empty or not, with the possession of the house and the rent book in her name, my mother could make a fresh start in building a home.

Homelessness left me in peace even longer this time. I graduated from university, married, and took up my career in the south of England. In September 1963 I became an administrative officer, Grade III, with the London County Council Welfare Department. Although I visited the vast reception centre for homeless people at Camberwell, which apalled me, as well as taking part in the London census of homeless single people in 1964, my major interest was in the problems of the elderly. My job was to manage about a dozen Old People's Homes. This was extremely absorbing but, after about a year, I had a stormy row with my immediate boss and decided to leave. I made arrangements for a job as a social worker with the Middlesex Welfare Department. However, the senior staff at the London County Council did not want me to leave and offered to promote me to Deputy Superintendent at the L.C.C. Welfare Office for the Homeless under Hungerford Bridge near Charing Cross tube station. I accepted this post and stayed with the L.C.C.

The Welfare Office for the Homeless was a really terrible place in which to work. It was directly over the Charing Cross tube line, next door to the main line station, and immediately under the railway bridge so that the noise was like that of a continuous earthquake. There was no natural daylight and the movement of trains brought down clouds of dust from the ceiling. Every day scores of men came in for free handouts. We took meticulous records of their histories and present situations and added this information to the tens of thousands of files we had already. The men were mainly living in lodging houses or sleeping rough and had heard on the grapevine that we might help.

Without being too unkind, the L.C.C. Welfare Department used this office as a retirement/rest home for its elderly, physically handicapped and sometimes recalcitrant local government officers. On the first day I met the person whom I was to replace. He stared at me grimly, asked me where I was brought up and when he heard it was Durham, said 'Another bloody Geordie down to steal the bread out of the Cockneys' mouths.' He was being transferred to another office where he would not come into direct contact with the general public.

There was a staff of seven. None had any training in social work or allied subjects and most had been Poor Law relieving officers in 'the good old days' and were waiting for retirement and their pension. The atmosphere was terrible and the general morale extremely low.

The aims and purposes of the office had not been substantially reviewed for more than a decade and it was my task to remedy this.

Our clients were often in the depths of poverty and despair. Many had recently been discharged from psychiatric hospitals or had come fresh from prison, very often for offences connected with drinking. Some wandered the country, hitch-hiking to find work or lodgings but were too restless to stay anywhere longer than a few months. Others had physical disabilities: the loss of a limb or tuberculosis. I remember a few who were deaf and others who were either blind or whose sight was poor.

Many were soldiers who had never adapted to Civvy Street and walked with straight backs and heads held high. Proudly they would show medals won on the North African front or in the Italian campaign. They talked about the 'old days' in the services when they really knew where they were. Now they marched from clothing handout to soup kitchen, into lodging house and reception centre and back to us for a food ticket or a free bed.

Quite a few of the men were still angry about what was happening to them. They were furious that just a few years before they had been married with children and a house and now they had nothing. Others were simply passive. They had lost any fire and were prepared to be downtrodden by social workers, social security officers or anyone who represented officialdom. They just did as they were told and this frequently meant being deprived of their legal rights.

Among the very saddest were the women. A home and a woman seem to go so much together and a homeless woman seems to lose all human dignity. In the midsixties the number of homeless women was very small. They were mainly elderly, dressed in rags and carrying vast brown-paper carrier bags full of assorted rubbish.

One was called 'Broadcasting Lillie' because she was so deaf that the only way of being sure to be heard was to speak very loudly into her old hearing aid, shaped like a BBC microphone. She was thin, scraggy and looked as if she was in her early sixties, but even she, like many of her friends, made a few shillings from the hungry men in the lodging house queues. She went around for a while with Weighty Willie and Steal-a-Horse Jake. They slept at the back of one of the park bandstands covered with newspaper and old cardboard. Willie weighed about twenty stone and could have put Lil into one of his many coats and never found her again. Steal-a-Horse was a miserable devil who was so called because he once did several months in prison for stealing a pony in the North.

I spent one wintry night with 'Mad Pat' in Trafalgar Square, alone with the lions. At four o'clock we both got soaked by the spray of the street cleaning machines. I was furious. She clutched her many carrier bags and railed against the omnipresent Goldstein family. 'They hound me. They persecute me every waking hour of my life. They have had me put away in a mental hospital for no reason at all for the last five years. Those Goldsteins are after me. Scratching my skin; pulling my hair; burning my feet.' Other homeless people would not go near Pat. They were afraid of her. She had been discharged from a large south London mental hospital a few months previously and had not slept in a bed since coming out. I heard later that she had been carried off in a police van after throwing milk bottles at passers-by. She went back into hospital for another long spell.

Trying to make the sixty year old Welfare Office more relevant to these men's and women's needs was very difficult. Could I possibly interest an ageing and untrained staff in providing modern social work care and a support service? I would not try to do so now but in 1964 and

1965 I almost broke my heart in the attempt. Those two years were two of the most important and informative of my life. My major interest had changed from old people to homeless single persons. It seemed to be a growing problem about which very little was known and in which hardly anyone else was interested. Newspapers would not print stories about it; radio programmes would not broadcast about it and social workers ignored homelessness and busied themselves with their case conferences.

The number of people sleeping rough seemed to be increasing and the general hostel facilities were abysmally Victorian. Visiting one of the large common lodging houses, where years before as a teenager I had been refused entry, was like walking back into the pages of Charles Dickens. They were human warehouses. My protests and careful reports were consigned to files and the two local government ripostes were, 'It used to be very much worse until recently' or, 'We are going to hand it over to another authority very shortly. No sense in doing much.' Interest was at a very low level and change took place very slowly indeed.

Homelessness was a peripheral concern. The Welfare Department was preoccupied with the elderly and the handicapped. Our resources were incredibly stretched to provide even the scantiest cover for those groups. There was no chance at all of getting resources to deal with the 'vagrant' and tramp who should, after all, be looking after himself, according to the official line. Successive governments and local authorities denied that there was much of a problem. 'Greatly exaggerated by a few well-meaning but misguided voluntary societies' was the line given to M.P.s asking questions in Parliament or the very few interested journalists.

This whole situation fanned my own considerable energy and anger. I frequently felt that there were only two intelligent people in the entire country who cared about homelessness: Audrey Harvey and myself. I had read her very impressive Fabian pamphlet: 'Casualties of the Welfare State', while still a student. I met her in 1965, grew fond of her; her immense commitment and exhausting energy. I supplied some up-to-date information for her important *New Statesman* articles, which gradually began to highlight the tremendous problems at the very bottom of the housing market. It was not just the Welfare Office, all the other services were so Victorian too. Churches ran missions on the Embankment to save the souls of the lost and fallen. Men stood singing hymns in the rain and were given a meat sandwich and a mug of steaming tea for their pains. Some winos boasted of being 'converted' twenty or thirty times. It was the easiest way of getting a new suit, money in your pocket and somewhere to sleep. Prodigal sons were always welcome.

Soup was the panacea for homelessness. It was possible to taste up to a dozen different varieties of free soup during a weekend. Hot ladlefuls were dished out to the hungry unshaven men by the River Thames. If they pitched a good enough hard luck story they might get a change of clothing or the price of a bed. There was no attempt to make a deeper social relation with the men. It seemed a very patronizing exercise.

I began developing a Tuesday club, which offered 'tea and sympathy' for skippers (sleepers out) and dossers (men in the lodging houses). The main point of the club, which was held in the waiting room of the Welfare Office from 6.00 – 10.00 pm every Tuesday, was to extend my own knowledge of and contact with the homeless men. I saw George Watt recently, one of the club's most regular users at that time. He gave me a long lecture on the complete ineffectiveness of the soft 'tea and sympathy' approach. The club ran for over a year and had a regular attendance of twenty to thirty men, who drank gallons of tea, sang songs, complained about prisons, the Salvation Army and the spike (reception centre) in that order. I became very fond of the men and grew to prefer their company and conversation to that of the staff. The club closed when I left the job.

Many came to see me during the course of each week. I helped them straighten out their social security tangles. When the National Assistance Board officers refused to pay them on the grounds of their being 'without a fixed address' I rang up and argued their case. Some of the men wanted to undergo alcoholism cures and I tried to get them places in various psychiatric units. Some hospitals refused on principle to accept meths addicts so I took their cases up with the regional hospital boards and later with the Press.

Geordie Hobson and Happy were two buskers who played regularly in the West End cinema queues and never missed a Tuesday, except when doing a prison sentence for drunkenness. Happy was very short and lively and probably the worst exponent of the tin whistle the world has ever heard. Geordie was from Durham and collected the money with an old felt hat and a long mournful face. He only ever smiled when Happy laughed. They had been together for years and years and loved each other. They either lived in an old lodging house or slept out in the Victoria Embankment Gardens.

Both were very heavy drinkers of cheap wine. As Geordie explained 'You have got to keep getting it down your throat. It is the only thing which keeps the cold out on a winter's night.' I would often see them swaying down Northumberland Avenue, begging from passers-by. They were real characters and a vital part of London. The police loved them; the casualty unit at Charing Cross, whom they were always pestering, loved them; the man in the tobacconist's shop across the way from the office gave them sandwiches from his own packed lunch.

They did not come in for a few mornings and missed a Tuesday club. I thought they were inside again until Geordie came to see me alone. He was very upset. One wintry morning, Happy, very drunk, had fallen under a bus in the Strand. He died instantly. 'David what am I going to do without Happy' he said and cried into a filthy handkerchief. He was completely lost and came to see me two or three times daily. I fiddled him some money to return to Gateshead and he left dressed in a nearly new Women's Royal Voluntary Service suit and I've never seen him since.

The club also made good contact with about a dozen homeless women. There were few facilities for them; nothing much in the way of day centres or hostels except those run by the Church Army and the large Salvation Army hostel in Hopetown. There was very little hope in Hopetown. When I visited it I was extremely depressed by its drabness and dismal atmosphere.

Everyone seemed to link homelessness with men. The women were largely ignored. Those who came to the office or club were very odd: Frannie usually came in about half an hour before closing. She clutched a big mug of tea as if somebody was likely to steal it and smiled silently through blackened teeth. She looked about fifty but was a good deal younger and lived with a group of winos and meths men on the south side of the river. She rummaged about in the dustbins for old vegetables and made soup on open fires. She begged for drink and slept with the men in derelict houses. For a few months of the year she would not appear by courtesy of the staff of Holloway Prison. On leaving prison she would look several years younger, fit, well and very

smart, only to return to the wino group once more.
'They're the only real mates I've got', she'd explain.
About a year later I heard that she died. There was a
single paragraph in the *Evening Standard*. I rang up the
police and they said she'd been found murdered, half
burnt by an open fire with her head badly smashed open.
I do not know if they ever found her assailant.

I tried to develop the day time office as a centre where
voluntary societies could get advice and direction on
homelessness. The staff used to visit voluntary bodies
who, with very little local authority support, were developing residential projects. I went to see the Revd.
James Martin, who was then working with Cable Street
Methodists, and the Revd. Denis Downham who was
drawing up plans for what is now the Spitalfields Crypt.
In those years, I watched the growth of the newly-born
Simon Community, soon to become the largest and most
influential organization in the field of homeless single
people.

The Welfare Office also became a centre providing information, not only to Audrey Harvey. We kept a vast
number of log books and statistical tables on our users.
There was very little help given but an enormous quantity of record keeping. Most of it was utterly useless. I
did some surveys of people sleeping out in the winter of
1964–5. It was in December, 1965 that I first became
very concerned about increase in the number of homeless women. At that time there were usually about eighty
or ninety people sleeping rough on Waterloo station.
Quite suddenly I noted that the number of women had
grown to fifteen or twenty at a time when the L.C.C.
were closing down facilities for them. I spent several
grim cold nights on the station making shy contact with
these multi-overcoated women. They worked mainly as
cleaners in the surrounding cinemas and theatres, and

then got pretty drunk and spent the rest of the night, often in pools of urine, on the hard railway station benches. To make matters worse, they were moved on periodically by the railway police, and deposited in the icy windswept streets.

My written reports about the increase in the number sleeping rough went unnoticed. London County Council policy was not to be changed simply by what was happening in Waterloo Station or in the Embankment Gardens. County Hall was a long long way from Geordie and Happy. It seemed that although it might be possible to make the Welfare Office a little more human and enlightened, the world outside would remain indifferent, and homelessness would continue to pass unnoticed.

Two things conspired to prove me absolutely wrong: one exacerbated the situation and caused large scale human suffering and the other cast a brilliant and lasting searchlight on that particular social problem area so that it would never be the same again. First, despite struggles at County Hall, the Conservative government insisted on implementing the London Government Act which divided the old L.C.C. Welfare Department into twelve separate boroughs on 1 April 1965, with very little thought about provision for the homeless. The new inner London boroughs taking welfare responsibility from the Welfare Department were ill-prepared to deal with homelessness. They had insufficient homeless family accommodation units; nor enough staff to cope.

This made me both very sad and absolutely furious. Hundreds of homeless families wandered around central London for months following the implementation of the new Act. Some families were given rail and bus tickets to outer London boroughs and authorities in other parts of the country, Scotland and Wales and told, 'You'll find somewhere to live in central London'. One woman who came to our office with her nine year old child had been evicted in the London Borough of Wandsworth. Her husband had disappeared with another woman and she had fallen behind with the rent. She had gone to stay for one night with relatives in Lambeth and when applying the following morning to Wandsworth was told, 'We are terribly sorry but you're no longer our responsibility. You are now officially a Lambeth resident.' Lambeth baldly told her that she could not be any responsibility of theirs and so she was stuck in the local government fly paper. I fixed her up with a hostel while her little boy stayed at our house. After a week she found a flat and settled down.

The situation was overwhelming. Every night in the railway stations, floods of families settled down with very small children in prams and carry cots. At one time the Welfare Office was receiving several families a day and getting stonewalled by the local authorities concerned. I spent hours screaming down the phone at indifferent officials. They were simply carrying out regulations which were themselves valve systems to protect scarce resources from being overwhelmed by a tidal wave of consumers. I have no doubt that some of those officers slept soundly in their beds and read excellent sermons as Methodist lay preachers on Sundays. At that time, I averred that the only way of getting real housing progress was to make every senior local government officer homeless for a month every year.

The Act also made the Welfare Office a City of Westminster responsibility. Our new masters mouthed platitudes and showed mild hostility to us rather than the bland indifference of the L.C.C. It is my belief that Westminster wished to close down the Welfare Office almost from the takeover in April 1965. It actually survived another four years. The office was an untidy embarrassment covering not only the City area but the whole of central London.

Homelessness received the searchlight in the shape of a rather peculiar and intense man who arrived at the office late one evening and parked his scooter outside. He was tall, lean and well spoken and pushed a grubby well-worn manuscript into my hand. Could I possibly check some facts for him? He had got my name from some socialist social workers I knew. I answered some of his questions and several days later met him in a Villiers Street pub and talked some more, this time into a tape recorder. I thought and heard no more about him. His name turned out to be Jeremy Sandford and the grubby manuscript was 'Cathy Come Home'. This play, screened three times on BBC Television launched a nationwide homeless families movement and did more than anything else to raise public consciousness and alter the map of homelessness.

By the time 'Cathy' was first screened I was working as a senior mental welfare officer with West Sussex County Council in the quiet seaside town of Shoreham-by-Sea. I was fed up to the back teeth with homelessness. I could not cope with the hordes of families in central London and what seemed the unending, one-sided battle with local authorities. There seemed to be nothing one could do. 'Cathy' changed much of that.

Over the next four years I escaped temporarily from homelessness; learnt a good deal about community mental health; started a playgroup for mentally handicapped children; a club for the older handicapped and made closer contact with my wife and two children. Occasionally I wrote about homelessness; came into contact with some discharged psychiatric patients sleeping rough in a South-wick bus shelter; took a young homeless man or woman home; but on the whole they were homeless-free years.

While studying for my Diploma in Mental Health at the London School of Economics I had the idea of writing a brief essay on common lodging houses. It seemed to me that their occupants were stuck on a large treadmill. I had stayed in several lodging houses as a consumer and was horrified at the Victorian conditions and the obvious physical and mental ill-health of their users, on whom no one had produced a report since Merfyn Turner's 'Forgotten men' in 1960.

Nick Grealy, then a colleague at West Sussex County Council, and I did a great deal of research and thought the report might make a pamphlet called 'The Treadmill'. I sent it to Ian Henderson of Christian Action, who liked it very much and it was eventually published in December 1969, simultaneously with an article in the *British Journal of Psychiatric Social Work.*

The report, tracing the development of the lodging houses, and life in them was a tremendous success. It triggered off a number of TV programmes, radio documentaries and newspaper articles and inspired the funding of a government research programme. I did the rounds of news interviews for several weeks and it all appealed to the 'public relations man' side of my personality; a side I do not like very much. Most importantly, 'The Treadmill' brought me back into homelessness. It persuaded me that I might have something important to give and that, due to my increased knowledge of both social work and mental health, this contribution might be substantial.

About a year after 'The Treadmill' was published I left local government. I left for several reasons. I felt that there was precious little room for imagination and creativity in that sort of social work and that there would be even less with the implementation of the Social Services Act, 1970. I left because I was becoming more heretical and *avant garde* in my approach to group work. I also left to go into homelessness. On 1 January 1971 I went to work for the tiny voluntary society called Christian Action which had published my first pamphlet. They had been making their uncertain way in the field of homeless single people for roughly four years and were then talking about expansion. I exchanged a solid career in local government with many opportunities, for another which had very few. I exchanged a regular and secure salary for an uncertain one of more than a thousand pounds less.

2

A COMMUNITY FOR HOMELESS WOMEN

My new job with Christian Action brought me to the turbulent centre of homelessness. Over half the voluntary societies were hardly on speaking terms with each other. Senior staff watched each other jealously, especially when government money was allocated. Working in a voluntary society was in complete contrast to being in local government. At Christian Action we worked on a shoe-string budget, in appalling conditions, packed like sardines in a tiny office. Most items of expenditure had to be carefully examined and pruned before they could be authorized. With West Sussex I had had tremendous resources but no real freedom, whereas with Christian Action we had immense enthusiasm and creativity but no resources.

One of the biggest problems was raising money for projects. The public would give generously for dogs and cats but not for homeless people. When we should have been pressing on with new schemes we were forced to spend time fund raising. We used to joke that if we had been a society for homeless pigeons then there would have been millions of pounds coming in.

Christian Action was founded by Canon John Collins in the 1940s to pioneer a concern by radical Christians for the poverty, suffering and injustice in the world. By the late sixties this had grown to the world famous Defence and Aid Fund, anti-apartheid and research group; the London School of Non-Violence, initiated by Satish Kumar; and the homeless side which was my primary concern. When I joined, Colin Hodgetts the new Director was attempting to guide the organization into more modern channels. At the beginning of the seventies,

Radical Alternatives to Prison joined Christian Action and brought in a new kind of aggressive and intensely committed energy which disturbed the more settled groups considerably.

I spent part of my time researching, writing and visiting other homeless projects. But by far the most important part of my work was with the Lambeth Shelter, Settles Street and later the Greek Street community for homeless women. The Shelter in Settles Street was a small house in the East End of London which it was hoped to develop as a centre for homeless alcoholic women. My first task was to provide a synopsis of the research which had been done there, and information about similar projects. There were no comparable projects in this country, and apart from notable exceptions like Spelthorne St Marys, Egham and St Mary's in Lambeth, the emphasis was on much larger communities for male alcoholics.

We appointed a warden and two staff early in 1970 and tried to get residents. Having read the complaints of probation officers and magistrates that there was nowhere to send women alcoholics one would have thought that this would have been very easy. In fact, it was quite difficult. Most of the chronic offenders in whom we were interested did not want to go into any sort of hostel on discharge from prison. I visited Holloway Prison several times and after four months we still had only three residents for seven single bedrooms. All probation officers and medical social workers in the inner London area were circulated with project information but the response was very limited.

Some women came for a few hours or days and then went back to boozing. Others were violent and apparently brain-damaged. But by August of the first year we had five residents who were 'dry' for months at a time.

Gwen, the oldest resident, had over 250 convictions for drunkenness and had been the terror of the inner London courts. She had lived rough for many years. Now she has been 'dry' for eighteen months with only two relapses and lives in private accommodation in North London.

These first five women increasingly ran the project themselves and we cut down the staff to one warden and a volunteer. The residents did their own cooking and cleaning. Most went regularly to Alcoholics Anonymous meetings which were of great value. During the first year, I had frequent meetings with both the staff and residents in which we discussed mainly the problems within the house.

Christian Action's own Lambeth Shelter was opened by the Archbishop of Canterbury, a near neighbour, in October 1967. It provided a home, in a small terraced house, for fourteen destitute women. Originally, it was a free night shelter and the women had to be out on the streets during the day time. The regime was quite stiff and authoritarian with a matriarchal warden. Gradually it developed as a community where the residents stayed longer, received more social work help and gradually took over greater responsibility for running the project.

My major tasks there were generally to supervise the social work staff and to run weekly groups for the residents. The Shelter, later to be made famous by Jeremy Sandford's 'Edna, the Inebriate Woman', had a friendly and permissive atmosphere. It housed a very wide variety of different women whose ages ranged from sixteen to seventy-three; the period of stay from one night to more than a year.

After the discipline and hygiene of Shoreham-by-Sea Health Centre I found the Shelter hard to take. It was a scruffy place. Although it was supposed to take only fourteen women, in fact there were often more than

twenty. They slept in the television room; on the landings
and sometimes even in the bath. The staff were simply
unable to turn people away.

There were major divisions within the staff. Two of
them were not on speaking terms and communicated
with each other through copious and illegible notes in
the massive log books. They had no common philosophy
and rarely met together to discuss what was happening
within the project or to settle differences. The early staff
meetings were terrible: some people said very little but
maintained an angry silence while others made the most
of trivial issues. However, the operation of a shift system
in which the staff hardly saw one another ensured that
the project worked.

Neither the working conditions nor the clients at the
Shelter would have been tolerated by a local authority
department. The residents were a difficult group including Irish and Scots girls who had left home for the
first time and then regretted it. Some of the older residents whom I had known in my Welfare Office days
were retired prostitutes and practising alcoholics. Some
were similar to the residents in the Settles Street Shelter
and had spent half a lifetime in Holloway Prison for
drunkenness offences. Periodically, they took off to sleep
rough and drink themselves silly, but they nearly always
returned, often lousy and injured. They had immense
character and dignity.

I remember Gypsy Rosie who stayed at the Shelter
when her man was in Pentonville, usually for stealing
lead from Church roofs. I have never met a man who was
'framed' as often as he claimed he was. Rosie's constant
companion during his absence was a bottle of cheap wine.
She used to smuggle it in late at night and drink it under
the bedclothes. She serenaded the other residents, usually
in the early hours of the morning, with a wide repertoire

of ribald songs. She was a ham. About fifty, with black hair, she dressed in gaily-coloured Romany clothes with gold rings in her ears, and played her part three times larger than life. When her man was freed they would leave the same night and hitch-hike down to the south coast. But underneath all that gaiety she was immensely sad and tearful.

Early in 1971 we started to get large influxes of young drug dependants. They were young in years but as old as the hills physically and mentally. Most were thin, sad and using large quantities of barbiturates. Frequently they would take overdoses and spend a night or two in the local hospital. About a half a dozen were on Phyceptone and regarded themselves as a superior race, within the drug world at least. They were very offended if I accidentally called one of the pill-takers a 'drug addict'. They were at least fixing (injecting drugs) and not just swallowing drugs.

One big problem was the large number of physically sick and mentally ill women we turned away for lack of room. Even though the house was stuffed full of homeless women, there was incessant knocking on the door and the police, probation service or local authority social workers telephoned trying to find beds for people. We turned away more and more women each month. There was a desperate need to find larger premises to house more women as well as to develop further the Lambeth Shelter's notion of a caring community. We wrote everywhere in an attempt to find new premises. The rejection letters: 'We are very sorry but the pressures on us are really so enormous that. . .', could have papered the walls of our tiny office. None of the London Boroughs nor the giant Greater London Council could find us a building in which to expand. Just when things looked most pessimistic, we were offered two possibilities. One

was in Bedford Road, Stockwell, where the London
Borough of Lambeth thought we might be able to use
a terraced house which was later developed as the Excell
House community by Radical Alternatives to Prison.
The other was the Theatre Girls' Club at 59 Greek Street,
London W.1. The large, five storeyed building had been
empty for over six months and the Club were anxious to
find financial backing and a new role for it. We looked
over it and became excited by its potential. I worked
out plans for a new style community which would
succeed the Shelter. We began to appoint a new and
lively staff who would be energetic enough to build up
new concepts in residential care. The atmosphere in
Christian Action became quite heady and there was much
talk of 'lighting beacons into the eighties'.

We were under few illusions about Greek Street as a
building. It was institutionally designed and had an old
Edwardian gentlemen's club atmosphere, both entirely
inappropriate to its new purpose. It was big enough to
house forty-five women and occasionally, like the Shelter,
many more. It was to offer beds to those who were
destitute. This would mean, almost certainly, that the
new project would attract many of the highly disturbed
street drug addicts and West End regulars, which most
other schemes vigorously kept out because they were so
troublesome. Could we cope with them where so many
others had failed?

All the fourteen residents in the Lambeth Shelter on
10 November, 1971 were transferred to Greek Street
and the terraced house was closed temporarily. For the
first few days there was considerable hostility within the
new project. The residents wanted to go 'home' to
Lambeth, and the staff could do nothing right. There
were floods of complaints about food, about the rooms,
the heating, the bathrooms, despite the fact that the

facilities at Greek Street were an improvement.[1] The staff too were very anxious. I had a strong personal interest in the future of the project. I had pushed hard for it and felt, to a great extent, on trial within Christian Action. Some of the staff thought the new building was much too big and impersonal and there were fears about running an 'institutional' project.

We tried from the outset to run the project on the twin principles of minimal intervention and non-selection.[2] Any woman who was homeless and destitute would be accepted if there were a vacancy. Christian Action provided social work resources: four full time staff on a rota (plus myself as the only social worker living in), two kitchen staff, a part-time maintenance man and a full-time volunteer. There was broad agreement among the staff about getting away from the hierarchical, interfering hostel regime.

I was interested in applying ideas of 'beingness', culled from Buddhism and gestalt therapy, to a residential setting. What would happen if people were not treated as problems to be solved? If the labelling that had taken place in the wider community was rejected? What would happen if a therapeutic community was set up where, in addition to having some kind of therapy programme like the Henderson Hospital (social psychiatry) or the Phoenix Community (for drug addicts), it was actually possible for people to opt out and yet remain within the building?

Residents in Greek Street could use prescribed drugs and no pressure was exerted to 'get them off'. They could come in rolling drunk and not be evicted. They could bring in their friends up to midnight when the doors were locked. The staff aimed at steering away from making dogmatic judgements about the residents' ways of living and yet remaining clear of collusion.

The first few months were packed with stress. A small

voluntary society, with slender resources, has to fill an empty project as speedily as possible for urgent economic reasons. This meant that forty-six residents were admitted in a matter of weeks rather than months. Such is the pressure for accommodation in Central London that we could have filled the building many times over. There was great trouble in working out the hotel side of the community, problems to do with laundry, catering and cleaning. Collecting rents was much more difficult than we had anticipated. Residents were expected to pay £5.85 a week for full board and lodging; about half the economic cost and upon these weekly payments lay the economic basis of the project. More than two thirds of them were unemployed and the local social security office paid. Many and ingenious were the excuses for not paying rent until, at one stage, nearly half the residents were paying either very irregularly or not at all. Residents who had the most difficulty in paying or excuses for not doing so were frequently those who functioned badly in other areas of the community; who were most often stoned or drunk. Christian Action then appointed a full-time social worker/administrator to ensure that the rents were paid regularly and to sort out the complexities of supplementary and sick benefits. He had a very difficult task and tended to be the Aunt Sally of the project and picked up a great many of the residents' negative feelings about both the project and the staff. It was usually he who had to tell someone to leave when their rent arrears were too high and to nag the social workers about the financial position of the community. Nowadays, an officer comes every Monday from the local social security office and everything runs reasonably smoothly.

Much more disturbing emotionally were the outbreaks of violence. During late December 1971 and January,

1972 there were many incidents involving pushes, punches and several split and bloody heads. Crockery and windows were broken regularly, chairs smashed, kettles and hot-plates bent and dented — there were a large number of overdoses, slashed wrists and faces until the whine of the ambulance became a common sound at our main doors. The place was overwhelmed with violence. The whole community shook with anxiety. Some residents were afraid of being attacked and several staff members were also nervous. I was attacked violently by an alcoholic resident after taking her bottle of whisky away and pouring it down the sink. She seized me round the neck and pulled me to the floor. I struggled with her under the dining room tables, knocking chairs and fallen plates about, while a dozen residents ate their lunches and watched.

The Shelter had never before run into violence on this scale and we did not know how to handle it. We had failed to allow for the immense effect the large, rapid influx of new residents would have in upsetting standards of behaviour within the new community. We had given birth to a *Lord of the Flies* situation. An immediate, rigorous taboo on violence was given at the Tuesday house meeting, which at that time all residents were expected to attend. Several women were subsequently evicted for punching and scratching and the whole atmosphere gradually calmed down. The enforcement of the taboo on violence created a deep rift among the staff. There were those who wished to pursue a more permissive and flexible line and others who felt the need for firmer and more disciplined ways of working. The gap was often so great that it was scarcely possible to have an effective dialogue. One group argued that the women in Greek Street were poverty-stricken, deprived and needed a great deal of love, affection and understanding rather than the psychological whips of house rules. Another stressed that the most frightening thing for people who had been in institutions for a long time was *not* to have any rules, lines and visible limits. This debate took up the lion's share of the staff time in the early months of the project.

We learnt a great deal about handling violence.[3] Residents threatening each other were goaded by on-lookers to resort to open conflict and any noisy confrontation tended to attract bored residents. Some hoped that the two or three warring women would stop just yelling at each other and turn to blows. We learnt to clear away the spectators first if there was no real physical danger to anyone. Sometimes it was possible simply to distract people. If a group were fighting in the lounge, I would switch off the lights or turn up the television volume. This would distract residents from their immediate preoccupation. If it was necessary to intervene physically, it had to be done very quickly. I got hurt only when I dilly-dallied and did not decide quickly on a course of action. Violence is always both exciting and frightening to me, and I believe, to most people. I always had to remember to breathe very slowly, pitch my voice low and evenly and act with assurance.

The staff had great difficulty controlling the use of drugs. Five or six residents were usually on heroin and Physeptone. Many others, especially the youngest, experimented periodically with 'fixing' and taking large quantities of barbiturates. The house rule was that all prescribed drugs were to be kept in the office medicine cupboard. However, several community members obtained Doriden and other drugs either by buying them in nearby clubs or, more frequently, and surprisingly easily, by registering with several different doctors. When a resident was 'down' and very depressed, her friends would 'help' by supplying liberal amounts of barbiturates from their own stocks. The staff were constantly being blackmailed in various ways to give out more and more drugs, 'You must give me more Tuinal, or else I'll kill myself.'

Illegal possession of drugs was a community offence but it was always difficult to discover the person responsible for pushing them as there was considerable loyalty between residents who frowned on 'grassing' to staff, reflecting their experiences in prison and psychiatric hospitals and their need to see the staff in an authoritarian light. When outbreaks of drug-taking took place, manifested by 'stoned' bodies all over the lounge, we imposed penalties more or less harshly and thoroughly lived up to this authoritarian image. Some residents would be anaesthetized in their beds during the day and noisily keep staff and others awake at night. On evidence from two or more people residents thought to be pushing drugs were asked to leave.

Eviction of anyone from Greek Street, no matter how reasonable the grounds, was always accompanied with much wailing and gnashing of teeth by the staff although residents who had been asked to leave and who subsequently returned, frequently saw their eviction as a positive constructive act. They considered that limits were being set to let them know that they had behaved intolerably and were 'being controlled'. But there was always the complaint that someone else had behaved even worse and 'nobody had done anything about that'.

In the light of these experiences, the original philosophy became considerably modified. I had begun in an optimistic mood of 'letting people be', of not asking for individual change, except in whatever terms the individual might see that. If someone wanted to lie in bed all day or to sleep with a fellow resident, then in so far as it annoyed no one else, it was no affair of mine. We were permitting a far greater measure of disengagement or non-participation than in most residential ventures.[4]

One abiding headache was an absence of intermediate sanctions. So long as we held on firmly to the idea of minimal intervention, sanctions were always a difficult and sore point in the community. What was our justification for intervening in the life of someone in the community? Did we see ourselves protecting other residents, ourselves, or the wider community? We usually gave ourselves a plain choice between simply admonishing those engaged in what we thought were destructive activities, or reluctantly asking them to leave. There were so many occasions in which something in between seemed more appropriate. At one stage we did introduce the idea of making people work in the kitchen, or clean out the bathrooms, as punishment, but that did not last long.

Margaret's difficulties in January 1972 epitomized the main difficulties in this philosophy. She was one of our longest stay residents and had come to the Shelter several years before as a young barbiturate addict. Her relationship with Jackie, another long stay resident, was very stormy and difficult and they rowed frequently. Margaret had showed great strength and persistence in extricating herself from most of the drug habits and the relationships of her youth. She became one of the most influential residents and was, at that time, the only one to have a weekly salary, for cleaning up. She had been very angry about being made to move from the old Shelter, her beloved home. She was also involved in long-drawn-out divorce proceedings involving the custody of her son. I and other social workers had sat in the divorce courts for the best part of a week, watching the last ashes of a bad marriage being bitterly emptied out.

At four o'clock on a cold January morning, she broke
down the office door with a large carpenter's hammer
and took all her own Tuinal tablets. She dragged herself
into the kitchen and left a goodbye poem on the large
trestle table.

> I feel myself slipping away,
> Nothing more can make me stay,
> I must destroy the physical me,
> So that my spirit can be free.
> I must go, so that I can find,
> My sanity in peace of mind.
>
> The memory of me that lingers on,
> Must not be a sad or unhappy one,
> I am not worthy of your sorrow,
> I could not live to face tomorrow,
> My heart is full of love for you,
> And sadness for my failure too.

She made her way very slowly upstairs and died outside
my bedroom door as a final act of defiance, or sorrow. I
found her thin pinched cold body at 6.30 a.m. that
morning.

She had already made several attempts on her own
life. In the few days before her death she had been in
several skirmishes over community rules. There was a
question of whether or not she was pushing drugs and
she had also been found with a key to the staff office in
her possession. She had described this as her 'insurance',
so that if she ever felt really desperate she could gain
access to the drug cupboard. We took her 'insurance'
away from her.

She had spent the last hours, in her own words 'very
goofed' (stoned or pilled) and had received tremendous

love and affection from the staff. I am wary of excessive affection in human relations. I feel that used without awareness it can begin rapidly to penetrate a hard shell which has become necessary for survival. In Margaret's case, I think that this penetration let in memories of past pain and sorrow which were too harrowing to live through.

For several days after Margaret's suicide, both staff and residents were numbed except for occasional, disturbing hysterical outbursts. People felt immensely guilty. Some said 'If only I'd died rather than Margaret' or screamed at me 'It was your fault that she died'. Jackie, her girlfriend, was distraught and sat in her room all day not wishing to see or talk with anyone.

The major gain was a real spirit of helpfulness which inspired many people. Before Margaret's death there had been very little community involvement but now we were going through a deeply disturbing experience together. Someone immediately volunteered to take on Margaret's job of preparing the breakfasts and cleaning. Residents helped to console their friends, worked in the kitchens and tidied the rooms. There was a spirit of real teamwork between staff and residents.

Barnaby Martin, the administrator at that time said that Greek Street was a project where the staff took total responsibility and the residents took none. With the help of the Advisory Committee we realized the truth in this. When we complained about being short staffed, one advisor replied that there were forty-five staff members doing nothing. I had been guilty of doing too much for our residents; asking too much of myself and too little of them. Most did little to help in the running of the community. In the first six months of the project, only five to eight residents were working regularly. The majority spent most of their time actually in Greek

Street. Some lay in bed all day and then kept the house awake at night with loud radio music and singing. The staff had got into a mood of fatalistic patience and suffering; social workers tend to suffer acutely from feelings of worthlessness. The suicide and the subsequent time of reappraisal gave us faith that it was possible to change things.

I realized that most of our residents would do anything to avoid taking on responsibility. Windows were broken regularly in the lounge but no one would admit breaking them. In their view, they were living in an eccentric, good-natured doss-house which involved them in only a very minimal way. There was little sense of belonging or of being 'at home'. There was a general habit of avoiding responsibility within the project of asking the social workers to solve all problems. One woman attacked me early in the morning with a carving knife. Afterwards she said, 'My mind is a complete blank, it wasn't really me that did it.'

We were searching for methods of coping with a population of six registered addicts; usually eight chronic alcoholics; an assortment of people with varying physical handicaps, epileptics, elderly prostitutes and diagnosed psychopaths. The great variety of the residents made us feel anxious. In the early months, this mixture was such a Molotov cocktail that we could only hang on. Later, as we learnt more about expressing our own feelings and began to clarify our own roles, much of this energy was channelled into house meetings, encounter groups and, more importantly, into informal gatherings and discussions. I began to throw responsibility at the residents. When people complained about the meals or someone else's behaviour, the staff tried, in a very informal way, to see that they also worked out some kind of solution. The key issue was food, the most pressing and tangible problem in a residential community. Weekly house meetings were dominated by interminable discussions about the meals. During the first few months all meals had been prepared for the residents by a cook. But the residents complained that they were either too hot or too cold, too spicy or not spicy enough.

Breakfast was the first meal that was left for the residents to prepare. Then we stopped preparing meals on Sundays and then on Saturdays and finally all weekday midday meals. Nowadays, this means that residents are responsible, largely without supervision, for all the meals except the weekday evening meal. Sometimes this system runs reasonably smoothly and at others it is complete chaos, but the residents have to sort out the chaos themselves. There has also been a much greater involvement in cleaning and washing up. In the early days this was entirely voluntary; after a few months we experimented with payment. Nowadays several residents are paid for work they do in the house including one who looks after the office and answers the telephone.

Social work at Greek Street had often been primarily a refereeing job and social workers had to be physically fit. A period of duty meant standing between the threats and counter threats of warring residents. Staff on duty had to spend most of their time in the lounge watching for signs of friction. Later, instead of rushing into potentially violent situations like firemen, they allowed residents to control themselves. If a resident threatened someone the staff left them to it but reminded them that expulsion from the community was the penalty for violence. The discipline had to come from the inside rather than outside.

Carl Rogers' books, and the weekly encounter groups which I joined were a very helpful release for the frustrations and tensions which residential work engendered.

I used to think that everyone was hounding me. I had a fantasy of being a tape recorder into which everyone, staff and residents, complained about one another as well as about the project. One or two residents used to dog me with their moans everywhere I went. Rogers preached openness and honesty as a way of helping people. In his books he advocated professionals throwing away most of their techniques and giving more of themselves. I nearly always tried to stay close to my own feelings in relating to both residents and staff, particularly when demands were being made. Very often the demands for changes of rooms, better and different food, and more attention seemed to conceal the very basic and desperate needs and wants of extremely deprived people. They frequently seemed to be saying that as they had been brought up in orphanages, and psychiatric hospitals which had left them feeling upset and hurt, I ought in some way to make it up to them. Quite often the extent of their need was frightening. There was usually no way in which those wounds could be healed and so I tried to stay aware and sensitive to residents and express my feelings honestly. If I felt intolerably manipulated, I said so rather firmly.

One major disagreement among the staff lay in the meaning of love. There were those, like myself, who saw love as involving the expression of both negative and positive feelings. I held that it meant staying true to one's self, in fact, the opposite of humouring people. If I love someone, I will tell them that I am bored with their conversation when that is so. If I don't love them, I might not risk the quarrel or argument. Other members of staff held that love meant expressing only positive feelings; that feelings of hostility and rejection should be repressed. This disagreement, which was discussed a good deal, but which remained unresolved, reflected two different outlooks on life and led to different styles of working. When one resident was asked what she felt about the project, she replied 'What project? There are really four, depending on who is on duty.'

One major staff problem lay in my own Atlas role. I had regarded myself as the chief problem solver in the project and was, to a certain extent, so regarded by staff and some residents. This meant bombardment with demands from the staff and residents, particularly when they were disillusioned. Frequently, I retreated to my room to meditate or simply to pace it tensely. More importantly, this role of mine hindered the development of skills and expertise on the part of the other staff members, it held back the development of their own confidence and growth. A few staff members greatly resented this strong man role. Their objections led to staff rows and crises in December 1971 and in January and later in April 1972 about my taking too much on myself; being too dictatorial and arrogant. Although I felt very upset and pressurized, these attacks had a great deal of substance. I learnt to discourage others from leaning too heavily on me and gradually to phase myself out of the community.

After the first few months I had less and less direct contact with the residents. I tried to take a more balanced overall view of the whole project, feed in new ideas about its possible development and give guidance to the staff. Since my departure I feel that the whole project has become more democratic; the staff have greater influence on the growth of the project and there has been greater participation by residents to the extent of having some say in the appointment of new staff.

The residents of Greek Street helped me to grow up. They enabled me to explore the extreme ends of my own despair, tiredness, anger and sadness. They always seemed much larger than life. Their sadness was more sorrowful; their anger was noisier; their despair was deeper. Often they absolutely infuriated me but almost in the next moment would melt my hardness and fury by some gentle gesture. Some would badger me for money, drugs or cigarettes and in the same moment bring a present for my small children, Stewart and Toby.

Rosemary (see Chapter Five) was having some kind of outburst in the lounge — throwing furniture about and screaming. Downstairs, several different noises could be heard: someone was crying; another newcomer was screaming loudly. I wanted to prevent Rosemary from breaking the windows and also to go downstairs to see what was happening. I touched her arm and told her to go to my own room. I spoke to her gently as she seemed dazed, but I was very angry. I hardly ever allowed residents into my room; it was the only retreat I had. She followed quietly. I gently told her to lie down and breathe deeply. After a few minutes she seemed relaxed and I said I was leaving. I opened the door and turned to see that she was just about to heave a heavy chair through one of the large windows. 'Don't you bloody well do that', I shouted. 'I don't care what you bloody well do in your own room, but you are definitely *not* doing it in mine.' She dropped the chair in surprise and fear. Her daze cleared and she was really back in the room with me.

Patsy had spent five years in a hospital for the mentally handicapped. She used to play the piano next to my bedroom and chose two o'clock in the morning for her virtuoso performances. I talked wearily to her; begged and implored her to go to bed, to play during the day. Finally, after several nights of disturbed sleep, I simply screamed and chased her up three flights of stairs to bed. She never played at night again. She provoked

considerable violence in the community by talking end-
lessly and noisily to the most vulnerable residents,
goading them to hit her. She was capable of a continuous
stream of words which drowned any response. The only
way to communicate with her when she was angry and
screaming was to put one's face about six inches away
from hers and also let rip at full volume. After a few
months' stay she settled down and was only really aggressive when her mother visited her. She later left the
community to move into private accommodation.

At times we had residents who smashed a large
number of windows; kept people awake at night; or fell
stoned over other people's meals. During February and
March 1971 we ran into particular difficulty. Ursula and
Ruth were especially disturbed and disturbing. Ursula
threw objects, usually plant pots, out of the window into
the street endangering passers-by and cars. Then she broke
a windscreen of a car in Greek Street with a large stone.
The police came in to see me and her. We considered
having her compulsorily admitted to psychiatric hospital
where she had already spent considerable time but we
were reluctant to do so although we had to consider not
only the community but also our responsibility for the
safety of people in the street. However she continued to
hurl plant pots into the street and we had to ask someone to come from the City of Westminster mental health
service who eventually admitted her to a south London
mental hospital.

Ruth presented a very different problem. She was no
real danger either to herself or to anyone inside or outside the project. However she had a long history of
chronic schizophrenia and had been in Horton Hospital
several times. She had had hours of electro-convulsive
therapy and pounds of sedatives. Normally she was the
brightest and most sensitive of women with a lively and

intelligent train of conversation. But quite suddenly she began to deteriorate very rapidly; she became very confused, absent-minded, wetting all over the floor, neglecting herself; talking non-stop in a very irrational way. She woke up all the people in her room and talked about her children. She woke up all the staff in the early hours of the morning to ask for change for the telephone. She became a major source of tension and potential violence within the house and people were very angry and disturbed by her. They had become used to the 'daft' members who always talked irrationally but the deterioration of an intelligent and sensitive person was too much to bear. Some residents, particularly those who liked her best, thought she was ill and so bit their lips and kept quiet when she came to talk.

Ruth's behaviour lowered the quality of life within the community, as well as being a constant source of irritation to me. She kept me awake for several nights by shouting and screaming in the darkened lounge. I had to intervene in a series of potentially violent incidents with people harassed to the point of physical retaliation by her barrage of irrational conversation. She seemed never to sleep and to be everywhere at the same time; appearing in the lounge; a few minutes later in the kitchen throwing carefully prepared vegetables on to the floor; and then screaming at people on the top floor.

Ursula and Ruth both posed the basic question of how much irritating and incomprehensible behaviour the community ought to tolerate. How much should it allow when it seemed that other people could not understand or moderate an individual's behaviour? Of course this depended on balancing the welfare of the individual resident with that of the entire community of which the individual was a part, as well as assessing what kinds of alternative facilities were available. This was always a very difficult question to resolve and the Greek Street staff meeting discussed Ruth for hours before finally deciding that she was too much for the community. The fact that it was mainly the other residents who were paying the cost finally swayed the decision. If Ruth had been in our own spare room at home, we would have dialled 999 within twenty-four hours. She could possibly be controlled by the use of phenothyazine drugs and, therefore, we called in the emergency psychiatric services. The young psychiatrist who came said that what was happening was due simply to her personality and that nothing could be done. He had heard her talking irrationally but unless he could see her throwing things about or trying to assault people, there was nothing he could do. However after I had talked to him about her for some time he agreed that she should be admitted to a mental hospital the same night.

The question of alternative accommodation and facilities for the residents has always been very difficult. Most residents have no home or relatives who will have them. In the majority of cases, we have been aware that treatment facilities were woefully inadequate or non-existent, and that a particular resident might actually have to sleep rough if we decided to evict her.

Asking someone to leave was always done with the greatest reluctance and in the first year of operation we asked only just over a dozen residents to leave out of a total of 248 individuals. Most of the evictions took place during January and February 1971. Many residents who were asked to leave because of violent behaviour or drug-pushing, have since returned and lived amicably within the community. Only three residents including Jean (see Chapter Three) have been evicted on more than one occasion.

In the original plan of the project we had envisaged

the development of a series of resources for the use of residents if they so wished. I had in mind yoga, meditation classes and encounter groups, and other members of staff had talked about encouraging hobbies and literary discussions. Such ideas were slow to bear fruit, largely because all our energy was going into solving management problems.

I ran several relaxation classes based on sophrology — a sort of gentle relaxation therapy — in which residents lay down and listened to prepared tapes. These classes were poorly attended, but I also used sophrological techniques on individuals who were tense and anxious. I used a great deal of re-evaluation therapy devised in the USA based on getting individuals to release areas of frozen emotion. I focused on certain incidents in people's lives and tried to help them to express fears and anger related to them.

There were two weekly encounter groups — one for the staff and the other for residents — which I ran. The staff group went on for three or four hours, but the residents' group was usually much shorter. The encounter groups were basically very flexible. Both were entirely voluntary and placed a high emphasis on feeling rather than cognition. Residents were usually much less inhibited than the staff. The staff group attracted a very large number of social workers, psychologists and others from the outside community.

In the residents' groups I sometimes used music and had people moving and dancing and trying to stay in touch with feeling. At other sessions I tried to develop an understanding of Zen awareness and meditation; of discovering how it was to be in the 'now'. It seemed to me that our residents were either focusing their attention and energies on past, hurtful events, or anxiously anticipating others which might conceivably occur, and that it would prove helpful to encourage them to focus on 'nowness'. They quickly understood this and would whisper 'now' to me at other times of the week. They were encouraged to feel their personal difficulties rather than to cut off; to cry and laugh if that was appropriate. This release of emotion moved frequently into the bounds of hysteria, and in leading the groups I had to develop a very gradual and gentle approach. In addition, there was a weekly staff meeting, at which we looked at problems of staff communication, and also a Tuesday house meeting which all residents were expected to attend that lasted between thirty minutes and an hour.

With the development of these groups and the increased confidence and experience amongst both staff and residents, the community settled down. Violence, either to objects or to people, became uncommon after March, 1972. The weekly residents' meeting was encouraged to discuss wider issues and to make more and more important decisions about running the community. Community problems were discussed not only at staff meetings, but also with the residents. These weekly meetings were still frequently interrupted by the screaming of several residents who had been diagnosed chronic schizophrenics in mental hospitals, but other residents showed considerable tolerance of this.

Residents established a pecking order. There were one or two who became the whipping boys of the community and others who saw themselves as semi-staff, particularly the small group who helped regularly with meal preparation and cleaning. They tried to come into the staff room frequently and to get on 'matey' terms with individual social workers. This gave rise to outbursts of jealousy, some of it in terms of sexual rivalry, as their friends thought that they were getting paid too much or too little attention.

Greek Street evolved a distinctive way of dealing with things. The majority of residents knew exactly where the boundary lines of behaviour were drawn. To outsiders our way of life often seemed infuriating, procrastinating and tortuous. The Community resented those like the police who tried to impose foreign and external systems upon it.

Quite regularly, residents would be admitted to drug dependency units, remand homes, mental hospitals and casualty units. Increasingly, it was other residents rather than staff who kept in touch with those individuals. After the first three rather disjointed months, residents did more together. If they had hospital or labour exchange appointments, they accompanied one another; they played chess and cards together, they sat up or danced to records until the early hours of the morning. Letters were written by the residents to friends outside the project and people rang up to keep in contact. As we came up to our first anniversary, a high proportion of ex-residents were returning to Greek Street to tell staff and residents how they were faring. Some people made lasting relationships and found fresh accommodation together.

One important and unforeseen development has been that of Greek Street as a day centre. A number of former residents, winos from Soho Square and street addicts use the project either frequently or occasionally. Sometimes they are a nuisance; they come in fighting drunk or stoned, to fix in the toilets. Sometimes they are professional pimps or drug-pushers, but on the whole the development is a good one. It may be that Greek Street will have to have a particular member of staff to take care of these day centre aspects.

The original outline of the project had envisaged a community of forty-five women of varying ages and difficulties who participated in its running and used a variety of therapeutic resources when they felt these were needed. In reality, Greek Street was a group of women who saw their main difficulties simply in terms of not having accommodation. I thought that some of them were grossly psychiatrically disturbed. Some had been in psychiatric hospital for long periods and wished to get away from this aspect of their lives. There was a conflict of viewpoints between staff and some residents. There was the staff need to see the residents as 'mad' or 'psychotic' against their wish to forget all about therapy. It was always difficult to see precisely who was lacking insight in any particular situation.

It is difficult to help people by intending to help them. To some extent the very intention of being helpful is destructive to the process of help. Most people who have been of help to me have had little intention of so doing. It is also difficult to separate that which hinders from that which assists. Most things which have helped me to grow came originally as negatives. One woman told me that my affection was not real. That shattered me for weeks, but I was able to use it as an immensely worthwhile and meaningful experience.

Most of the real help at Greek Street is from resident to resident. Advice comes on settling in, on house rules, comfort and even first aid assistance, on the psychology of the various workers. The help arises spontaneously out of the process of living together. Social workers and other staff are used more frequently on an advisory than an emotionally dependent basis. They are asked for travel directions, for help in unravelling the mysteries of the supplementary benefits system, to make appointments at outpatients units (a high proportion of residents are receiving treatment of one kind or another). Social workers tend to chat informally in the lounge, pass on messages from the outside world; dish out pills from the considerable armoury in the office cabinet.

Much of this new relaxation and sense of community came from learning, very slowly, to be ourselves. Learning that quite often we would make mistakes and misjudgements but that infallibility was not only impossible, but undesirable. I remember having a tremendous argument with Jean on the evening of her first eviction from Greek Street. I accused her of pushing drugs in the house. She denied this as adamantly as ever and said that the two young residents who had reported her were 'dirty rotten grassers who have just got it in for me'. I told her that she was an idiot if she expected me to believe that there was nothing more in it, and that she would have to leave that night. She said, 'You can't do that. You're just being bloodyminded and unreasonable.' I realized that she was right. I *was* being bloodyminded and for the first time in my life it was all right to be so.

REFERENCES

See also

1   David Brandon, 'Adventure in Caring' (*The Friend*, 14 July 1972).

2   David Brandon, 'A Community for Homeless Women' (*Social Work Today*, 14 June 1973).

3   David Brandon, 'Violence and Survival' (*Residential Care*, April 1973).

4   Dennie Briggs, Stuart Whiteley, Merfyn Turner, *Dealing with Deviants.* Hogarth Press 1972.

JEAN

Jean is tall and thin. Usually she looks scraggy and much older than her years. Her face has a very sad quality about it and her eyes look vacant which is occasionally very disconcerting. Somehow she communicates violence even though all her movements are languid and her voice is tired, flat and monotonous.

She is very intelligent and a great manipulator of social workers. She had one stormy four-hour session when she tried to blackmail us for more drugs than had been legally prescribed. Besides telling me how bloody-minded I was, she tried to grab the drugs from the office cupboard, kicked one of the social workers and ripped the log book in two.

I find it so much easier to talk about my problems nowadays. There was a time when it was just impossible. If the psychiatrists brought up the last three or four years of life with father I'd shut up completely and I still cannot talk freely about sex. If they ask me about sex, and they usually do, I shout or throw things at them.

I don't know my birthplace except that it was in the south of England. My father comes from an extremely wealthy family. Unfortunately he is a psychopath. He isn't merely a psychopath but it seems he's got schizophrenic tendencies as well. I found out from one psychiatrist why, when I'm in a very bad mood, I'm always homicidal. It's the one thing I've inherited from him: my temper. It's unfortunate for me.

He was a very peculiar person to say the least. Sometimes he was really good, like the last time we met. More often he was like a bull in a china shop. If he didn't get

what he wanted immediately he would be violent. Once
he locked my mother in the larder and cornered my
sister and me and just hit out at her. I escaped and hit
him over the head with a chair. It didn't knock him out
because I was only ten.

He very rarely hit me — my mother and sister yes —
but seldom me. He knew what kind of person I was.
Once he hit me but unfortunately for him it was a
Sunday and the carving knife was lying around. I picked
it up and said if he came any nearer me I'd stick it in
him. I'm not frightened of him now that he's in a mental
hospital; I just feel sorry for him.

The funny thing is that he worked regularly. He was a
taxi driver while we were children. He went out looking
for custom every day of the week. It was my job to make
sure that the taxi was nice and clean inside for all the
customers.

Life was a constant flit from one place to the next.
We lived at Hastings and then moved to Northampton.
We moved to Scarborough and then on to York where
we stayed for several years. In my early years we seemed
to be always on the move. Nobody ever liked my father.
He upset everybody and then we had to move on.

My mother never hit back at my father, even though
he treated her very badly, because, to be quite honest,
she hadn't the guts. Until about a year ago I idolized her.
I thought she was a pretty decent person — kind, and
with all the qualities a really good person should have.
About a month after I left Borstal I found out exactly
the type of person she is. She doesn't care a damn about
her family. She ignored me while I was in Holloway and
St Martins. The only person she cares about now is her
little son Adam, who is only four. I've hated him since
the day he was born.

When I was coming off drugs she left me to look after

him. He was screaming his head off and nothing I did made any difference. I changed his nappy several times and made him up three different bottles none of which he would touch. I rang my mother who was working at the hospital — she's a psychiatric nurse — and begged her to come on home. She wouldn't and my mind burst and I couldn't take it any longer. I tried to throttle him and at the same time suffocate him. I held him by the throat and threw him back in the cot and shouted, 'To hell with you. I hope you're dead.'

A psychiatrist said to me later that if I had killed him they wouldn't even have been able to get me for manslaughter. You see I wasn't in my right mind. I'd just done cold turkey off five grains of heroin. I couldn't take any physical or mental stress. Looking after a baby was just too much.

My mother's been the only person in our family that I've got on with. My older sister Christine and I have always quarrelled about everything. She's always said that I could commit murder and get away with it. She is four years older than me and never shown me any decency. Whenever I go home she says exactly the same thing, 'you won't be here long on drugs; you'll be dead before the end of the year'. There's no love lost between us.

I can't remember very much before my fifth birthday except for some fighting and rowing. My mother had gone out and I was hanging on the gate waiting for her to come back. I saw her in the distance with what looked like a roll of fur fabric under one arm. Closer to I saw that the roll was squirming and wriggling about like hell. Then I saw it was a puppy, just what I'd always wanted. She put it on the kitchen table and it was like a ball with a tongue at one end and a tail at the other. I've never seen anything so funny in all my life.

My early life had some moments like that but on the

whole it was fourteen years of absolute hell. Quarrels between Mum and Dad. Squabbles between relatives. Mother's brother hated Dad and made no secret of it.

The first thing I can remember with absolute clarity was the day at fourteen that I left my father. Before then is mostly hazy. A psychiatrist told me that it was due to memory blocks because there were things I didn't wish to remember. Some pretty bad things must have happened and I was cutting them off. I've tried to get through to them. I've tried in various groups to get through to my subconscious but never succeeded so it shows how deeply embedded it must be.

There are whole periods of my life I just can't remember. Sometimes they just began with taking too many drugs. Others because I got into a dream — it happened quite often as a child. I've had too many knocks on the head from my father. I used to suffer a lot from fainting attacks. My mother would be talking to me and I thought it was the weekend but it was well after. She'd say I'd been going around in a daze for nearly a week. Maybe its connected with the epilepsy although the first fits didn't really start until I was fifteen.

I remember odd bits about being at school. In some ways I detested it and in others liked it. I always came near the top of the form but I rarely had friends. My father made sure of that. Any girls coming to our door were either chased or told that I was out. I passed the eleven plus and Dad didn't want me to go to grammar school. He said I'd become a snob mixing with other snobs and complete idiots.

My mother finally decided to leave him when I was fourteen. I said I'd leave home if she didn't; I'd already run away twice. We left him and he came after us. To my mind he looked very pathetic. He told Mum that he was going into a mental hospital for two weeks' trial and he would stay on longer only if my mother agreed to come back to him. She refused.

Life was much quieter without him. I got four 'O' levels a year late because of all the drug-taking. I was on both H and coke (heroin and cocaine). I'd been on drugs since about fourteen because it was so easy to get them in York. I was creeping out at night to a club called 'The Frying Pan' where you were supposed to be sixteen to get in.

There were a lot of pills at that time but not much H and coke. I was occasionally helping behind the bar until it was closed down by the police. I could get as much meth (methadone), coke and H as I wanted. The pushers had every drug imaginable from a warehouse which was easily broken into. Even the D.D.A.s (drugs classified under the Dangerous Drugs Act) weren't locked up.

I started on heroin — skin popping it (injecting under the skin). I knew about injections from my mother and could get syringes through her, whereas for most people it was difficult. After a few months I went on to mainlining (injecting into veins) and this was even before we left my father. I was smoking hash pretty regularly and every other weekend would come down to the West End to get supplies of drugs. At that time H and coke were a £1 a grain.

Just before I went into hospital it was ridiculous and horrifying. I'd moved away from my mother down to London and had a pad in Notting Hill Gate. I was taking twelve grains of H, ten of coke and about twenty amps of meth. I could get the drugs from two doctors who were later struck off. This pad was full of addicts, about eight to a room. I was in a hell of a shape. Physically, I looked about fifty. I couldn't talk coherently and kept collapsing on my feet. I had a whole year of this until the end of 1968 when meth was taken off the market.

I was registered at this time with the Westminster Hospital drugs clinic and they advised me to go back to see my mother. At that time the clinics were giving you precisely what you asked for. The first three days after registering was hell because they couldn't give you more than two or three grains of anything until the urine tests came back.

I went back to York and the clinic gave me a script (prescription) to take. I hitched up with another girl and had completely run out of drugs by the time I arrived. Mother was disgusted with me and I did look pretty grim. I was starting to get withdrawal symptoms. She said she knew a doctor where I could get some stuff (drugs). We staggered to a bus stop with me holding on to her so tightly she was almost falling over. She took me to a psychiatric hospital just outside the town. It was horrible, just like a prison. The psychiatrist was the worst I've ever come across. Even though he told you home truths it was done in a nasty spiteful way.

It took six nurses to get me into bed. I fought them all the way. They gave me an injection which was probably Largactil. They wanted to get me off meth which had messed me up. It was months since I'd had a proper sleep because I was using so much I couldn't get to sleep. I was down to six stone and they were giving me medicine to make me eat. The nurses were given instructions that no matter what time of the day or night it was, if I wanted food it was to be supplied.

They had no idea of how to treat addicts. I and the girl who hitched with me were the first they'd had apart from a few pill-takers from the University. They kept me unconscious during most of the time I was there on what this bloody awful psychiatrist called his 'sleeping cure'. You can tell how wonderful it was because the first thing I did on running away to London was to have a fix. Running away was farcically easy. The other girl and I threw our clothes out of the ward window and watched carefully to see whether anyone was coming and ran all the way down the drive.

I've been an in-patient in mental hospitals several times since then. I was in St Martins for several months. It was quite a good experience because they got me off drugs completely. I went there after being picked up by the police for two cases of assault on them and illegal possession of hash. I went into Holloway for eight days and then got out on bail.

I've been in trouble with the police since I was just fifteen. The first time was for shoplifting but I don't even remember what it was that I stole. I got two years probation that time. Next time it was for illegal possession of Chinese H (heroin). Probation is no good for me. If they tell me not to do something and I want to do it I just go right ahead. They've realized now they may as well get used to it.

The probation officers have given me some right lectures, particularly about using barbs (barbiturates). I was on them for over a year and nearly lost the lower part of my leg as it was gangrenous. I was in Charing Cross Hospital for two weeks and it scared me rigid. I promised myself I'd never touch them again. My present probation officer is busy making a list of all the addicts who have died recently. That's a horrible thing to do. She keeps nagging me and saying that's what's going to happen to me. I don't like to think about death.

The second time in St Martins was a real disappointment. The psychiatrist who had me knew nothing about addicts at all. She would barge her way in at the ward meetings and in her strong Hungarian accent say 'Pleese tell me what is a feex; what is a screept?' She did that with me once as I was telling my life story so I threw a glass ash tray at her. They discharged me after some weeks drug free and I was sent by the probation officer to Oxford for recuperation. I came up to see her in London and at the same time visited a doctor with whom I'd been registered. I wasn't really after stuff but met an addict friend in the waiting room. He advised me to spin a story about using such and such an amount and how I didn't like clinics because they weren't helpful. It was just a lot of rigmarole to get the stuff. On the basis of this the doctor wrote me a script for 35 amps of Phyceptone to be cashed in Oxford.

I cashed the scripts in London and stayed on at Oxford making a weekly trip for the script and to see my probation officer. That went on for about six weeks until I got an angry 'phone call from my probation officer who wanted me to come down to London urgently as she had found out everything.

I found somewhere to stay and registered with the clinic at St Clements but was also getting drugs from various general practitioners. I went in to St Martins who were sick of me. I got very aggressive at one of their group meetings and threw things around. I was very upset at having a 'phone call from my mother who was accusing me of everything short of murder. I was taken to a locked ward where all the patients were schizophrenics. Everywhere was locked. They put me in a side room and locked the door. It would have been all right if they hadn't locked the door. I screamed and banged against the door. Shouted and threw the bed about. They came in and put me in the pads (padded room) which was awful. I screamed for three days. Every time the psychiatrist came in I kicked her; I hated her so much. I wanted to go back onto the addicts ward. The nurses on the locked ward were disgusted and said I wasn't a person who needed their kind of psychiatric help and I shouldn't have been there. Most of the patients were demented and there was no one to talk to.

Eventually they practically threw me out. The probation officer got me into a Salvation Army hostel near King's Cross. It was quite good really for a short stay place. While I was there I had about four or five different doctors. I was using a hell of a lot of barbs and writing my own scripts from a doctor who was struck off shortly afterwards. A week before he went to court he wrote about twenty scripts with a difference of a week between the dates on each one. They were for Nembutal rather than Tuinol which gives you really bad abcesses.

I was actually working around this time – as a typist. I had learned to type at night classes. The drug habit was really bad and the clinic, who didn't know the half of it, asked me to go back into St Martins yet again. I went in under a false name and you should have seen their faces when they saw who it really was. A few days later they threw me out. They said I was being violent which just wasn't true. I went straight across London to St Clements and was taken in. I was stuffed full of Largactil and feeling very poorly.

I went back to work on leaving St Clements. At first I was typing and later operating calculating machines. My foot was playing me up yet again and I was in poorish shape physically. I packed the job in and went down to the Dilly (Piccadilly) to get some stuff and got picked up by the police. I spent ten months inside. Five weeks in Holloway and the rest at Bulwood Hall Borstal, Essex. The food at Holloway was completely inedible, at least at Bulwood you could eat it. There was a certain amount of work – I was in the flaskmaking factory – and a certain amount of free time. On the whole the borstal was fairly helpful, although there was a lot of very boring routine.

You worked at the same time; had your meals at a certain time. Same thing day in and day out.

When I left that borstal I had not had a fix for over eleven months. My downfall was going home to see Mother. I didn't want to go home but I was practically forced into it by social workers. She accused me of fixing which was a downright lie. I couldn't discuss anything important with her. She just wasn't sensible. I came back to London very upset and angry. I got myself stoned the way some people drown their sorrows in drink. At first I stayed with some friends and then with the Simon Community in North London while I waited for a place at Christian Action. I came to Greek Street in November 1971.

Until the end of January 1971 I was scoring very heavily (getting a lot of prescriptions) and then the clinic put the script up. They gave me 4 amps of Phyceptone daily and now I'm on that and two nightly Doriden to help me sleep. In the same month I was chucked out of Christian Action for hitting an addict called Penny Black who is now dead. After two or three weeks they let me come back again.

I've never bothered to think of my life as a whole. It's been one massive up and down all the time. Mostly down. Even if I try to plan it doesn't usually work out so that now I just wait to see what happens.

I've never been able to express emotion very easily. I feel it but can't show it to others. I'm afraid of getting hysterical and out of control. I did it once at Bulwood and had to be left completely on my own. No one to see me except the doctor for a week. I just cried until I was at screaming pitch. I felt rejected by everything and everybody and hated Bulwood.

Drugs were my outlet. My former probation officer put it like this: 'Jean', she said, 'Your sister has been a cryer all her life. She cried about the brutality you both went through. You couldn't do it that way so you had to have another sort of outlet — drugs.'

I can't imagine myself married and I find sex very embarrassing. The truth is I've got rather Victorian views about it. That's just me. Not that I know much about either sex or marriage — the last time I contemplated going near a guy was when I was about sixteen or seventeen. Most people behave like animals; they're just out for as much as quickly as they can get it. Most men just want chicks for bed, they're not interested in your mind or personality. All they want is sex. They don't know the meaning of the word love.

I wouldn't like to fall in love. Its hypocritical. People say they're in love and all they're after is sex. I don't agree with it. Some chicks fall in and out of love like getting in and out of bed. The only emotion I really know is hate. I've got to where I can hate people pretty badly but I rarely get to where I can like anyone, and as for anything beyond liking, well . . . I don't think I can ever care deeply for anyone. It's to do with all the times I've been let down by my family: my sister, my mother and my father — right from being a very small child. There was nobody I could rely on — do you see? Everybody's always let me down.

4

PEGGY

Peggy was a very large, sixteen stone plus, plain woman who looked much older than her years. Her face was big and sadly expressive. Her speech was depressed, but extremely colourful. When talking about personal problems her voice dropped to a halting, almost inaudible whisper. She was full of stories which bubbled with cockney humour. Her hands and wrists were covered with the traces of deep slashes from suicidal attempts.

Peggy, big, depressed, humorous Peggy is dead now. She was found dead in her room at the discharged prisoners' hostel where she went after leaving the Lambeth Shelter. She had taken too many sodium amytal tablets, which she used as a sleeping aid. No one can tell whether it was suicide or not.

In one of our last sessions, she asked that whatever happened to her, to make sure that her life story was published. It might be of some help to someone. . . .

My father was a lorry driver. Mother was very small and Jewish. I was the oldest child — Rosemary was two years younger; Brian came two years later, and then a gap of eight years and Debbie.

When I was a baby my mother wouldn't have anything to do with me. She was going to put me into a Dr Barnardo's Home, but my grandmother wouldn't let her. So I was brought up with my grandmother until she died. Then at six I went to live with my mother. Even in those days I was always running away, anywhere. The police used to find me but I didn't know my name. Eventually, my uncle would come and collect me. I used to wander for miles.

I hated my sister Rosemary. If she was brought down in the pram to see my grandmother, I'd push the pram away and leave it somewhere with her in it. When I was thirteen I pushed her into the Thames by Wapping Steps.

It was horrible going back home after my grandmother died. I always felt terribly unwanted. My mother used to hit me over anything. Luckily, the war started and I was the only one evacuated, but she kept following me and bringing me back. I went to two places in the depths of the country and then she got bombed out and stayed in Somerset. I had to go and join her. Every week, well, that's a lie, every month we had a different father. Dad was away in the army. I think that's why she doesn't like me now because I can remember. She was on the game in the transit camp.

I got on very well at school when I went, which wasn't very often. When we lived at Dagenham she started me and my sister at school and got a job. Then she decided that eight year old Peggy would have to stay at home doing the housework and looking after her four year old brother. The school board kept writing to her, but she just burned the letters. I came up in front of Stratford Juvenile Court and went away on a fortnight's remand. When they asked my mother why I didn't go to school, she said, 'I can't make her go, she's beyond control.' And I got three years approved school.

I was happy there. The school was at Whitley Bay in Northumberland. Mum wouldn't have me home for the holidays and Dad was still in the army. I was the baby of the approved school, terribly spoilt and I never got punished. Then I passed the eleven plus and went home but my mother bundled me into Southover Secondary Modern. She wouldn't send me to a grammar school, she couldn't afford the uniform.

At fourteen I refused point blank to go to school: I had already learnt everything that they could teach me so I just wouldn't go. The Juvenile Court gave me another three years approved school. I kept running away from Bosden Hall in Gloucester, where they placed me. Eventually, they just refused to have me back. I was put into Winston Green Prison (Birmingham) until I was sixteen. They gave me three years borstal training and so I went to Aylesbury. I smashed up so much crockery and broke chairs and tables so they sent me to Holloway for a medical report which sent me to Broadmoor. I was there nine months until my father found out that I shouldn't be there at all because no court had authorized it.

I went home and returned to high school. I passed all my exams and could have gone to University. I've been in and out of hospital and prison ever since. Every hospital I've ever been in, except Broadmoor, I've run away from. At Broadmoor you don't stand a chance. Even if you get over the wall, they call out the dogs and the army. Once I found a ladder and climbed over the wall on to the path beneath. I was so afraid of being chased by the dogs that I rang the admission bell and said, 'Here I am.'

Shortly after leaving school I started sleeping with a Polish seaman — really my only man friend in all these years — although I didn't like him much, I had a baby boy, Peter. While I was in prison, or psychiatric hospital, his aunt took care of him. He was a quiet baby. I was a good mother and never slapped him once. He died at eight years old of meningitis. Afterwards, I ran away to Liverpool and landed up in hospital.

During this period, I was very, very aggressive. I was really mad. I used to break doors down, smash all the windows. They didn't know what to do with me. At nineteen I had a leucotomy in West Park Mental Hospital. I don't remember much of this period. I don't smash windows any more. I didn't turn into a cabbage, which is what most people do who have had this operation. They just sit and stare. I've been back to West Park since but there was a sister who kept reminding me about what I did and what I wouldn't do now, so I ran away.

I was a terrible fighter in those days. If anybody said anything to me I'd slosh them and the nurses would grab me and stick me in the pads. I nearly murdered a girl once. She kept calling me a prostitute. It was in a hostel and I got my hands round her throat so they sent me to Cane Hill Psychiatric Hospital.

I've been in Holloway lots of times, but always on remand. Holloway's a dump. If you're not a criminal when you go in you are when you come out. It's grim in the Obs (Observation Unit). You go in there and if you haven't fought or struggled they place you in an ordinary side room. If you fight, it's a room with nothing in it except a mattress and you. They never come in to you and push the food through a hole in the door. You get your breakfast at nine, luke-warm tea in case you throw it over somebody; web-footed forks, bladeless knives and picnic plates. I used to make them furious by shouting for soup. You clean the landing. You get dinner and are locked in for two hours.

Early afternoon there is occupational therapy; sewing and knitting. Then you are locked up at 3.30 p.m. for the rest of the day and night. Nothing to interest you and no exercise. Holloway is so noisy. Until midnight, you get women calling out, 'Sandra, I love you. All my love and I'll see you in the morning.' The officers bawl out 'Shut up'.

While I was in there, I didn't talk to anybody about

my problems. I never do discuss my personal problems with anybody. I feel such a fool. I just sit and say nothing. All the while I was in Broadmoor I used to see the psychiatrist three times a week. He never used to get a word out of me. He'd get exasperated and yell, 'Lost your bloody tongue.'

For treatment they always gave me E.C.T. (electro-convulsive therapy) and Largactil. The electric shocks used to terrify me. I've had them so many times in Broadmoor, West Park and Horton. I always had them when I sauced a nurse or swore. I think I was given them as punishment because they knew I was frightened. Punishment rather than treatment.

I liked Broadmoor the last time. There's a lot of social activity. You work eight hours a day, but get a proper week's wages. Not like Holloway, 22p a week. You get £3 − 4 in Broadmoor. Then there's choir; auditions for the play; bingo; whist and dancing. There's something on every evening. I used to paint in there, in oils. Mostly landscapes or Spanish dancers. I edited and did drawings for the *Broadmoor Chronicle*.

I was detained 'during Her Majesty's Pleasure'. I had to get used to the idea of being there. Everybody was mad except me, so I sat under the table behind the piano. I wasn't mixing with that lot. But when I got used to it, it wasn't so bad. If there's a fight, both parties get punished. Even if you don't think it's fair at the time, it is really. You might have said something even if you didn't punch anybody. They send you over to the re-fractory block. You have to sit in with the staff and are not allowed to smoke except at certain times.

I can't count how many suicidal attempts I've made. I must have taken overdoses on dozens of different occasions. It's usually to do with my mother. Once when I had seen her she treated me as a complete fool and kept calling me 'mad Hannah'. I ended up taking two hundred Mandrax and going into St Thomas's. There's a great conflict between the part of me that wants to die and the part that wants to live. I need desperately to forget sometimes. At eighteen I took to drink. The trouble with alcohol is that you always sober up and have to start drinking again. My boy-friend was buying me whisky. Then, later on, I was mixing with a Maltese ponce in the East End. I used to keep an eye on his prostitutes to see if they had any extra men. I always said I'd seen nobody. At that time, I was drinking a bottle of cheap wine a night.

My father was an alcoholic. He doesn't drink now. For years he drank heavily, but it didn't really help. I still get very depressed about my mother. Sometimes I wake up in the morning and can't think of anything except her. I hate her. I can't do anything about her. I tried killing her once, just before I went into the Maudsley (psychiatric hospital). I borrowed a rifle and threatened to shoot her. Now, I know the only way I can get rid of her is to get rid of me.

I don't only overdose. I've slit myself with bits of glass on hundreds of occasions. I used to break windows and use the glass to cut my arms. Nowadays, I break milk bottles and eat bits of the glass. Once I cut my stomach and the intestines were hanging out. I'm very self-destructive. I get so depressed it forces me to take things out on myself. My physical health is also poor — I've had osteomyelitis badly. I have had bad bronchitis and breathing problems. I have periodic trouble with vomiting. They've operated on my stomach several times and I don't know what the doctors were doing. It didn't do me much good. My epilepsy is a worry. I was knocked down by a car when four years old, and I've had fits ever since. Nowadays it's one every two or three months. I fall over and can't remember anything about it. I get no warning and just sleep for four or five hours afterwards.

I like a little bit of security. When things get too much for me I can just go to the police station and say I've done so and so. Then I get sent to prison. For example, if I get upset and want to take an overdose, I need to be able to get in somewhere to stop myself doing it. So as an insurance, months previously I fiddled my social security book. I've already done something now. I had a book in November which lasted me until February. During Christmas week I went to the social security and said I'd lost it when I hadn't. So I've had four extra weeks out of that book illegally. I could turn myself in any day. This time I will go down for two years.

Usually I go into Holloway for fiddling social security books. Last November it was for stealing a stethoscope. Originally, I'd been in hospital in Sussex and they'd messed up a minor operation involving a catheter. I stormed up to the doctors in London, having discovered a piece of catheter inside me and the doctor wasn't interested. I was furious and stole his stethoscope and ophthalmoscope. They remanded me in prison and I ended up with two years probation.

I don't know what will happen to me. There is nothing I really want. I expect I shall come to a sorry end as my mother always said I would. Life is just too much. I'll die quite soon and make a vacancy for someone else. I had a housemother once who frightened the life out of me talking about reincarnation. 'You're so wicked,' she'd say, 'you'll come back for ever more.'

I'm just too institutionalized. I don't manage by myself. I'm so used to having my meals at a certain time; going to bed and getting up at set times; being told what to do. I can't act for myself.

I've never even seen one of these M.W.O.'s (mental

welfare officers) they talk so much about. And as for P.S.W.'s, (psychiatric social workers) they're not much help. They just ask where you are going to and give you the train fare. They don't seem to care where you're staying. When I left West Park Hospital I had nowhere to go and no one seemed to care. I landed up in the women's reception centre.

I've had dozens of jobs in my time and always worked fairly hard while I've had them. Farm work, shop work; my longest job was as an assistant in an old people's home in Islington. I used to get drunk every day. I was there for three months. I hate to get stuck anywhere. 'I've been a rover all my days', but love has not been good to me.

All my real loves have been animals. My first dog was a bitch. I didn't know the difference. When I brought it home my mother said, 'I hope that's a dog'. I said, 'does it look like a rabbit?' So I got sent flying. I've had a few dogs since then. I've got one now. Animals are easier to understand. I'm always putting people on pedestals. When they fall off, which they always do, I lose interest. I don't know why I do it. I've given up making real friends — it makes less to worry about. I made a friend in Broadmoor once, but she fell ill and I used to worry myself sick about her. In the end I'll either die or end up back in Broadmoor. This time I don't think they'll ever let me out.

5

ROSEMARY

Rosemary was Greek Street's first resident. She came there before the big transfer from the Shelter. She is very thin with a face scarred from razor slashes. She seems to flinch away when you talk to her. Her hair is cropped close and her voice is soft and halting. She was in charge of the first aid kit and helped to stitch up the residents who were not injured badly enough to merit the casualty department of a hospital. She seemed very eager to please except when she had intense bouts of depression and hysteria. During these periods it was very difficult to make any real communication. Then, we — the staff and the residents — were 'all lined up against her.' No amount of reassurance seemed to work. She left Greek Street over a year ago. She re-visits occasionally. As far as I know she is living, reasonably happily and drug free, in private accommodation.

I was born thirty-four years ago in Lincolnshire. My father was a surgeon and I got on fairly well with him although he was always pretty strict. He had heart trouble and an extremely bad temper. He wouldn't accept illness in the family. As far as he was concerned he'd enough to do with his own patients. When we were ill we just had to get on with it.

I never came up to his standards. We were both musical. I remember he'd had a car crash and stepmother graciously allowed me to go and see him. I'd been singing in a festival and had failed to get top marks, only a credit instead of a distinction. He was furious, 'After all I've done is that the best you can do?' It made me feel a great sense of failure.

I had a twin brother Peter and a sister Elizabeth who was three years older than me. She was a totally different person. As adults we both qualified as nurses. She was always abruptly in control and very much *the* nurse whereas I got involved with the patients to the point where it hurt. She died of cancer about four years ago.

My own mother died when I was only four. She had been a nurse before marriage. She was not pleased at having me. She only wanted a boy and Peter was enough. She tried to kill me by throwing me out of a window. Father married again soon after her death. Stepmother was absolutely brutal. She resented my loyalty and devotion to father and made my life absolutely impossible.

She really hated me. I remember her saying it was always dark when I was at home and the clouds suddenly lifted when I went to boarding school. She thrashed me many times. I didn't like meat as a child and she would starve me until I ate it. I hated her. I was scared stiff of her. I had an obsession that she had a gun in the cupboard and was going to shoot me. I would lock myself in the bathroom and sleep in the bath.

Peter and I were devoted to each other. We played endless games together although we went to separate schools. When we were very small, stepmother went to the education people and said she wanted a severe school for both of us, where the discipline would be hard. I went to a Church school in Darlington. I hated it. They punished us by religion. If you didn't do something they sent you to bed with bread and water. We learned hymns for punishment but that hasn't turned me against religion.

At fifteen I went to Peterborough Grammar school. I was very rebellious and naughty especially to stepmother. She was quite sure that something was wrong with me. She'd already had me to the child psychiatrist when I was only eight. He said there was nothing wrong with me and it was my parents' fault.

My migraine started whilst I was at Peterborough. I used to be sick all the time. Father wouldn't help. The headmistress said I had to come as a boarder if I wanted any G.C.E.s so I went as a boarder. I only got three passes.

I left school at seventeen to do fever nursing. I'd stayed on an extra year to mature but it didn't make any difference. I did the fever nursing at Brookfields Hospital, Cambridge. It was very hard work. Like my father I was a perfectionist. Neither of us was ever satisfied until our work was at the topmost level. After two years I left to go to Addenbrookes Hospital to do my S.R.N. Peter was at Hammersmith Medical School to struggle like mad for his degree. I was having acute depression and migraine but he told me to 'hang on whatever you do'. Peter was a tremendous support to me.

I couldn't seem to find a middle course and still can't. I'm either terribly depressed or frightfully high. When I'm high I've got a terrific sense of humour which went down well with the patients. I was engaged twice whilst at Addenbrookes. I didn't love either of the men. The first one was an airman. That fizzled out because I wasn't happy. I broke it off. The second time was to a university student called Sam. Again I was nervous of him and got the psychiatrist I was seeing to tell him that it wouldn't work on psychiatric grounds. I said to the doctor, 'Please get me out of this mess. You've got to do something.'

Just after I qualified I left Addenbrookes. I went on holiday with Peter and a friend to Montreux in Switzerland. We were all in a car and had a bad smash up. They were both killed outright and I just sat there and looked at them before losing consciousness. We had been driving along when another car cut in front of us on a mountain road. It made us swerve violently into the path of another car. I went into hospital with severe brain injuries, fractured skull. I've had brain storms which result in my wrist-slashing and window-breaking ever since.

I was in that Swiss hospital with various injuries for six months. I don't remember too much about it until I returned to Addenbrookes. I did staffing at first but had to give it up due to brain seizures. They queried whether the fits I had were epileptic — petit mal — I kept passing out without warning.

I saw a senior neurologist and went into the Atkinson Morley Hospital where they decided I had got petit mal after all. I used to have the fits about once a month but I never quite knew what happened except suddenly I'd be lying on the floor. People didn't want to upset me so they didn't talk about them.

It was while I was at Addenbrookes that I started razor-slashing. I got desperately tense one evening so I used the razor on my wrist until the desperation passed away. I did it in the bathroom and cut the inside of the wrists. It wasn't an attempt at suicide. Afterwards it was very sore but that was a punishment for having done it. I needed stitching but very few people knew about it. I wore very long sleeves to hide the cuts. I'd recently got a Sister's position at Addenbrookes but obviously now I had to leave. I couldn't carry on even though the sleeves covered the slashes. Not long after that razor-slashing became a regular habit. It didn't really hurt at the time. It was as if I gave myself some sort of anaesthetic.

I felt the need to get out of the country completely so I got a post in Belgium, with a nursing agency. I was put in charge of a unit in Brussels which cared for psychiatric and neurological patients. I spoke French fluently as I've always been interested in languages.

I was in Brussels for a year before I collapsed. I had been taking tablets by the score, mainly Doriden. I got them from the clinic to help with the general tension. I had a lot of patients with brain tumours and one death after another. I was full of obsessions that dead people were running after me. It was quite ridiculous. I was taking night sedation by day. Eventually I was up to thirty Doriden daily.

After some time, the Professor in charge realized that I was in trouble. I told him about the drugs. I had been very popular with the patients. The staff didn't like it as the patients kept asking for me when I was off duty. I couldn't stay there so I left for a second clinic in Brussels where I was for just under a year. It was run by nuns. As a matter of deliberate policy, I was not in charge. I got very upset and emotional because one of the patients committed suicide. I felt it was partly our fault, particularly that of the sister in charge who could have done much more.

I was using both Librium and Doriden at that stage. The sister discovered about the drugs, had a fit and asked me to leave. I returned to England and went to live in a bedsitter in West London. One migraine was coming after another. I took a lot of pills and told lies right, left and centre. My landlady was very good and said, 'hang on and I'll do what I can'. So I went out to various private nursing jobs. I began to give up completely and was going from one hospital to another. They simply said that they couldn't understand why someone with my training, experience and intelligence should be coming to a psychiatric hospital and sent me out again.

I felt pretty hopeless. A week before my period I would go berserk. I was never quite sure what I would be likely to do. Sometimes it meant razor-slashing; on other occasions hysteria and window-breaking. My life was one long trek to various mental hospitals. It had started with a visit to Belmont shortly after I qualified as a nurse. I was there nearly a year and couldn't walk for nine months because of paralysis. They said it was due to nerves and I'd have to conquer it.

I went to Hellingly Hospital for severe depression. I had E.C.T. but it didn't work. For about two weeks it cleared me and I felt on top of the world and was writing letters to everybody and thinking that nothing would ever go wrong again but then I hit the ground with a bang.

I went to the Maudsley as a day patient but they weren't terribly optimistic. They said that there was not an awful lot they could do but they would do what they could. I went into St Lukes, Woodside, and the professor said 'if you can't get her better in three weeks we'll have to ask her to leave'. So I left.

I spent some weeks in Oakwood Hospital, Maidstone and went to Spelthorne St Marys for a year. I was admitted there by way of St. Mary's Hospital, Paddington, after taking an overdose. I knew the Spelthorne nuns very well because I was the matron at their junior school for over a year. They had refused once because they didn't think they could do anything. It was right out in the country and specialized in taking drug dependants and alcoholics of all ages. I tried to escape several times because they treated us like children of about two and a half years old. We had to go to occupational therapy; you couldn't handle your own money. If you wanted to go out it had to be with a nun. I was very unhappy there. I had one bout of hysterics after another. I was crying a lot of the time. Really I got very little treatment. They said I'd become too dependant on them. What hurt me most was that they told the magistrates later that I'd been a damned nuisance and a constant source of trouble to them. They said nothing about this while I was there.

The trek continued to Horton psychiatric hospital. They allowed me to go out after a time and help at a small nursing home. For some reason I took one of the doctors' prescription pads and forged a prescription and took it to the chemists where I got caught by the police. I was sent to Holloway prison on remand for three weeks. Oh God, I'd rather die than go to Holloway again; it frightened me to death. Mainly it was the acute disgrace I felt at being in there at all.

I was seen by the head doctor who said, 'I'll do what I can but you shouldn't be in here at all'. It was at the time of the mail strike so everything took much longer than usual.

A visiting psychiatrist from a drugs unit came to see me and asked whether I would like to go into his hospital. I would have done anything to have got out of prison. The prison had taken me off Doriden but I had the most awful side effects and withdrawal. It was simply indescribable. So I went to St Martins hospital. From the beginning I liked the staff but I didn't like the group therapy. The consultant psychiatrist came in one day and asked if we were all happy. I shouted loudly, 'No'. He pinpointed me and went on and on. So I went out of the room and smashed a window.

I teamed up with another nursing sister who was a fellow patient. She said she couldn't stand it any longer and needed drugs badly. We had an arrangement that if either of us went out we would get drugs by registering with various doctors. I went away for a weekend and was so stoned that I had to be brought back. I tried to tell the ward sister about everything but she just got very angry and said she would have me sent back to prison. As a response I took about eighty Doriden and was admitted to a general hospital where I hovered for some days between life and death. I think they'd even signed the death certificate.

When I was returned to drugs unit the ward sister said, 'Look what you've done to me. Are you proud of what you've done?' They all said I was a hopeless case and discharged me. I had been put on two years' probation for the prescription forging business. I saw the probation officer very regularly and he contacts me very often. I was homeless and had nowhere to go so he tried Christian Action first and they said they couldn't take me. In a few days they changed their minds and I came to stay at Greek Street which in those days was a hostel for foreign students holidaying in London.

Initially I got on very well. I had been discharged from psychiatric hospital as hopeless and unhelpable. But here, where there were no nurses or psychiatric supervision at all, I did very well – didn't slash my wrists, overdose or break windows – although I was taking large amounts of Doriden to keep myself under. I had a very good relationship with both the students and the young couple who ran the hostel. The husband gave me a friendly hug in the morning and listened occasionally to my fears. Just lately though, things have got pretty bad. I've broken lots of windows and I've had a police caution about that. I've been doing a lot of overdosing and slashing my wrists pretty badly. I don't know what's going to happen to me. I've been registering with four or five different doctors and getting lots of scripts for Doriden. I have been taking thirty and forty every day, which is about my highest ever.

The other day I went to tell my own G.P. about this because I couldn't get drugs from other doctors. I like him to a certain extent but he talks jargon like all the rest. He sent me to St Thomas's to see if another of those crazy fools could help me. The psychiatrist wanted me to go back to hospital but I refused very firmly. He said I wasn't bad enough to be sectioned (compulsorily admitted under section 26 of the Mental Health Act 1959).

I've never been helped by being sent to mental hospitals. That's been proved time and time again. They've always ultimately written me off. They can't help me. They can't touch me. I've got to help myself but I'm not sure how. People could help me but I don't see any reason why they should. They can help me best simply by caring but I find it difficult to believe that their caring is genuine. I've made an awful mess of my life. The only time I really enjoyed was my training. I was so much absorbed in the worries of the patients and so needed that I had no time to worry about my own problems and difficulties.

I don't really know about the future. So much of me lies heavily in the past. I think about the car accident and wish, long for Peter to be back, to comfort me when I'm feeling low and depressed. I think a lot about a girl who committed suicide here about two months ago. I feel I could have done something to save her — to stop her from dying.

I don't know what will happen to me. I don't think I've got much longer to live. If I keep playing around with huge doses of pills I must destroy myself quite soon. I don't want to get married. I couldn't care less about it. I'm not interested in sex and never have been. The very idea of dressing up and putting on lipstick and cosmetics is a lot of nonsense. It repulses me completely. I do need someone to care about me. It doesn't matter whether it's a man or a woman. I think Tom (one of the staff) cares. All the residents tease me about him. So long as that gives them pleasure it doesn't worry me. I'm not in love with Tom and I'm not chasing after him.

I want to be of some use to people. There have been times in my life, particularly with the dying when I know they've needed me and I've felt very good about it. I want to be able to help people rather than have them help me. I am grateful for the help I'm given but I don't like it.

I realize that I'm to blame for most of what's happened to me. If only I'd behaved differently. If only my father had been different toward me. I don't like finding fault with him now he's dead. He just asked for too much and I wanted desperately to give him it but I couldn't rise to the heights. He gave me very little affection and a bloody good belting time and time again. He and my stepmother made me feel a complete failure.

My biggest fear now is that I shall be sent away from here. You can reassure me. You can go on and on until you're exhausted trying to convince me that it's all right but try as I will to believe you I can't be convinced. I want to believe in your affection and caring but I don't know how.

About a month after this interview Rosemary was admitted to a mental hospital in south London. Previously she had been seen by a psychiatrist who had written to us, 'I have formed the opinion that she was a chronically depressed intrapunitive, aggressive psychopath and that placement in a long stay hospital would be the best way of helping her.'

She asked to see me rather urgently when she returned from psychiatric hospital where she had been for three weeks. She leant toward me, her stiff angular face scarred with slashes. I could see the razor marks even through her black stockings. She got into that rigidly hunched pose that she always uses when most depressed and agitated:

'David, I must tell you, but you're going to be very angry. Some of the stuff I told you on that tape just isn't true, not true at all. It isn't true that my father was a surgeon, he was only a general practitioner. It's not true that I have 'O' levels or that I passed my S.R.N. I failed my G.C.E. completely but I just don't like people to think that I'm stupid. I took the first part of the nursing examination but not the second, because that's when I went into Belmont Hospital with the paralysis. Even worse than that there never was any Peter, I simply never had a twin brother at all. He was a pure invention. There was no car accident and no death. I just wanted to be dramatic. I got to the state when I believed that I had a twin brother. It would have been nice to have had one to comfort and to reassure me. I have to invent another world.

'Most of the other things I said were true. Only after I left home I spent most of my early twenties in mental hospital or as a matron at private schools for boys. Since I left my parents I've not had a home at all really. This place (Greek Street) has been the nearest thing I've had to one. I sometimes miss the privacy and long to be wanted. To be quite honest I don't think I could cope with the demands people make on you in most homes.

'I am very sorry I lied to you. It's been on my mind ever since.'

6

THELMA

Thelma was a grandmotherly person who looked like the portraits of Elizabeth Fry which still adorn many Quaker Meeting Houses. She had a quiet, sometimes rather tired courage and warmth and often sadness rippled over her face as she spoke, especially when recalling incidents in which she has let people down badly. She was a lovely person. She seemed to be obsessed with gaining other people's respect and love, allowing them to lean on her ample form but in the end, unable to meet the demands completely, having to cut and run.

Thelma became the mother of the Shelter and was specifically referred to as 'Mum' by the younger residents. In the weekly house meetings — the focal point of the project — she had considerable influence and could control the meeting with a word.

About Easter 1971 her world collapsed, or perhaps she smashed it open. She was working at an alcoholics unit and the project leader on whom she had relied heavily, left. She eventually recovered from this blow and began to concentrate her energy on the Shelter. But she was torn in two directions: her desire to leave the confines of the Shelter and become independent, and her wish to stay and help others and fulfil her matronly role. In the end she told people that she had found a flat, borrowed some money and one weekend, secretly packed her things and left.

I was born 71 years ago in Nottingham. I am now a grandmother with eighteen grandchildren and five great-grandchildren.

When I was only three my father and mother separated

and he went back to Canada. I remember him very well, he was a fishmonger, a kind and tender man and the most loving father anyone ever had. My mother had committed adultery and fell for a child and my father could not forgive this. My mother was also a wonderful person, but I blamed her for the break-up of the marriage, although I was only a kid at the time.

There are thirteen children in the family and I am the oldest. My mother had them by three different men. I have one sister who is two years younger and eleven half-brothers and sisters. Only three are still living. One died of cancer when he was eleven. Bert hung himself at the bottom of the stairs when he was only thirteen.

When Dad went to Canada, the other man came to live with us. He was a good man, hard-working and kind. He was a hawker by trade and my mother helped him in his business. My sister and I were unhappy. It was our own fault as we were still thinking of our own father and we couldn't take to stepfather, even though he was very good to us.

When I was nine, my sister and I went to live with grandfather. He was a fishmonger and he had stalls and markets all over the Midlands. We lived there until he died when I was twelve. He was a very nice and just man. It was heaven there. Then we went back to mother.

I lived with my mother until I was twenty-two, then I got married. That was in 1922. In the beginning we lived with parents-in-law. My husband was working on the Corporation cleaning the streets. He gave that up after a few years and went in for haulage contracting. He had a hired horse and cart, and gradually, through a lot of hard work, built up quite a sizeable business. We started a family. The first child was a daughter and then followed two sons, Thomas and Sam.

It was a very good marriage and he was a good man

right up till the last ten years. In 1957 he picked up with another woman, which I couldn't believe. He went away from home to live with her and gave my elder boy power of attorney to run the business. After six months the other woman left him and he became a sick man. He had a cardiac failure and developed cancer in the neck. I still wouldn't have him back, but my two sons prevailed on me. I agreed on the condition that he shared a bedroom with one of them. I swore I'd never forgive him and I never did. It ate into me; I tried to forgive him, but I finally just couldn't.

My husband died in May, 1967. He had been sick for a few years and bedridden over the last twelve months. I still liked him, but I had lost any deeper affection. If he had ever made love to me I should have thought he was thinking of the other woman.

Six months after he died, my youngest child, Sam, was killed in a motor crash on the M1 on a foggy day. That was the beginning of me being as I am now. Sam was my life. I loved him. I loved him more than either of the others and I think that's why he was taken away; to punish me.

I took his son Sam then. I had him for about twelve months. When he was sixteen he wanted to go into the navy. When he left home, I gradually lost control over my emotions and had a very serious breakdown. I stopped bothering about myself or anything. I went into the City General Hospital for psychiatric treatment and was there three months. After discharge I returned home, but took ill after a fortnight and had to go back in once more.

I went in voluntarily, but seemed to be losing my nerves. I was ready for being mental. I was seeing things. I had visions of rats crawling over me. My husband and I had a spinney at the back of our home and we used to watch the rats and the squirrels. I could see those rats both day and night.

I still see my son Sam sometimes, even though he's dead. He's been to me since I have been here (at the Christian Action Shelter). The first time was when I was living with my daughter. I stood by the bed and felt his hand on my shoulder, just as clearly as if it was yours. One night I woke up in a cold sweat and heard his voice say very distinctly, 'My Mum, pack it up — stop it'. I think he was talking about the delusions. Since I've been here he's even walked with me in the streets. I think he's with me all the time, but sometimes I'm more aware of it. Maybe I'm being a fool, but I can't help it.

I was really no better when I came out of hospital. They gave me electric shock treatment. I couldn't get out quick enough, although they were good to me. I don't like doctors and I won't call one even when ill. A short while after discharge, I had delusions again about the rats. I became physically paralysed and lost the use of my arms and legs. I lay in bed, I was living alone, you see, and went without food or drink for two days. No one knew I was there. My daughter found me. She insisted on me going to stay with her.

My family was very good to me. At first I was bedridden and needed nursing. I was staying in Susan's — my grandchild's bedroom — and she was having an argument with her sister in their bedroom about whether the window should be open. That made me feel sick because I was responsible for them having to share a room. For weeks this sort of bickering went on and one day I overheard Susan saying to her Mummy, 'How much longer do you think Nan is going to stay?' And I thought they wanted to get rid of me.

While I was ill, the family sold my bungalow. That was the worst thing they could have done. That place was my whole life really. I was angry and hurt because no one had discussed it with me and because it was my independence. I started to look for a flat when I was a little better, but nobody wanted an elderly person, especially one that looked ill. One day, I told my daughter a lie, a big lie. I told her I'd found a flat and would be moving out within a few days. She was rather worried and tried to persuade me to stay. I refused. She offered to help me move, but I refused because there was no flat.

The following day I got on the first train and went to Liverpool. I don't know why I went to Liverpool because I didn't know it at all. I stayed in a Salvation Army hostel for a few weeks. It wasn't a bad place, you did get a clean bed. But there were imbeciles and mental cases and all that there. I cried for six weeks solid until I didn't think I could cry any more. When I got my new pension book I went straight off to New Brighton because the weather was getting warmer. No one at home knew where I was.

After a few weeks I travelled down to Brighton in Sussex. I slept out on the beach with the hippies and stayed there for most of the summer. The hippies looked after and protected me and I gave them some food. At night they loaned me a sleeping bag. The first time I met them I was having coffee and a flask of soup. One hippie came over and said, 'That smells good'. So I gave him the soup flask and it was returned empty. I got to know him and his friends very well. They were marvellous and their morals were very high. They were like angels to me.

The only income I had was £5.10 from my retirement pension. You'd be surprised just how well I managed. I'd buy a loaf of bread, half a pound of butter and probably a quarter of beef and that made a reasonable meal. I had no cooked meals at all. I slept out under the stars for all those months.

I saw a lot and learnt a great deal. I learnt to be much

more tolerant which was a thing I never was before. That was the time I realized I should have forgiven much more. I became more understanding and compassionate. People used to come and tell me their problems in a hut on the front, even the meths drinkers.

Towards the end of the summer, I moved to Southsea. Someone said it was nice down there and you could sleep on the beaches. I met up with two of the hippies who had been in Brighton. I slept out there until the end of September when the autumn was starting to blow in and so I came up to London. I heard that there were women's hostels for about £3 a week and then you had £2 over for extras. I thought I might be able to get extra from the social security but I couldn't do so, having no fixed abode.

The first two nights were spent in a small private hotel near Victoria. Then I slept out in Green Park and was questioned by the police. They said I wasn't the usual sleeper-out and if I stayed there I wouldn't be molested. They said I wasn't to go over into St James' Park because a lot of roughnecks and drug addicts were over there. In the morning, I went into Rochester Row police station and asked the sergeant if he knew of a place I could get a bed. He 'phoned up places all over London. Everywhere was full up. Then he said the only place he could get me into was the Christian Action Shelter. If I couldn't get in I was to come back and he would put me up in a police cell.

The Shelter was so full I had to sleep the first two nights on armchairs in the television room. After the first night, I asked if I could stay a few nights and then return to Nottingham. A few days after that I was walking down Tottenham Court Road and saw a job going at the Grill and Griddle: woman wanted to help chef in kitchen. I started a few hours later and I'm still at the Shelter.

Part of my stay here has been good and part very bad. The first few weeks were awful because I heard a rumour that you could only stay for two weeks. I didn't know what I was going to do when the time came to leave. Also, I was still completely out of contact with all the family and that was really depressing me. I didn't know how anybody was.

I felt suicidal. I walked over Westminster Bridge three times with the intention of putting myself in the water. Each time something seemed to pull me back like a hand on the shoulder. Two days later I did the same thing. I talked with the staff at the Shelter about my depression and they said I could stay until I got on my feet. This really took a whole load off my mind.

I gave up my job at Forte's some weeks ago and went to work as a cook/housekeeper in a men's alcoholic hostel. Right at the beginning, I had talks with the men and they told me their troubles. Their troubles were damned sight bigger than mine.

Three weeks before Christmas, I renewed contact with my relatives in Nottingham. I felt much more on my feet and had a bit of money. I spent twenty pounds on clothes to look reasonably respectable and went home for the day. My son met me at the station and took me to see my daughter who gave me a cold reception. I'd told her I was going into a flat when I left Nottingham. I'd told her a lie and she couldn't forgive me, although she fully understands now. I didn't tell them I was in a hostel. I just told them I was with Christian people. I wasn't very happy that day, there was a cold atmosphere. They were hurt as they'd spent a lot of time and energy trying to trace me through the police and Salvation Army. It was my grandson who broke the ice. He's only nine and ran into the house and shouted, 'Look, it's me Nan'.

After this I kept close contact. I phoned them every other night and wrote frequent letters. When you have a close family, like mine, you feel the loss of contact very greatly. Towards my family I had always been rather too generous. I'd give my grandson a bike, anything he wanted, but I wouldn't do that now. Since my stay with the hippies and at the Shelter I see it as a waste of money and material. I was always trying to impress my grandson; to keep his love. It was rather pathetic, you can't buy love. I was always afraid he'd go elsewhere for his love – so whatever he asked for I gave him. It was very wrong and I ended up by spoiling him.

I've got rid of a lot of the depression. The alcoholics unit helped me a lot. They look on me as a mother figure and I feel happy in that. Mind, I've had some bad times. One of the residents, Ernie, had left a family of three sons and it had been playing on his mind. When he was young, his mother had left him three times. One day, when I was preparing to leave – putting my hat and coat on – he took them away from me. He said, 'You're not going to leave me again Mum, you're staying here'. He put his hands on top of the door and banged and banged with his whole body and cried out, 'Oh my God, she's going away again'. I was heartbroken and a little frightened. I got past him eventually, but it shook me up. Later, he looked very sheepish and couldn't do enough for me. Now we've become good friends.

I feel I'm needed at the hostel. I can do a little bit of good with these men when they come in. It's like having another family. I want to stay there. Soon I shall move out of the Shelter to share a flat with Mary in Camberwell. I like Mary very much, but she is a bit domineering at times and it may not work out. But in the long run, I know that things will be all right. I found myself much more, you see. If I'm in trouble, I can ask for help.

I regret many things in my long life. The event I most regret is being unable to forgive my husband for his adultery. It grieves me deeply that he died without forgiveness, and all those years sleeping in another bedroom. He was a good man. We had 35 years of very happy married life. I never thought he would go off the rails. I just couldn't believe it.

I've learnt an immense amount from these last few months. I am a much more understanding person. I make more allowances for others which is why I understand the young kids in the Shelter. A lot of them have not got a mother or are not in contact with her. They look on me sometimes as their mother and I try to help them as a mother would.

Before I lost my son I was wrapped up in him. I had no love to give to anybody else. I lived for him and him alone. Before, I could never have lived alone, but now I can. I like the community life. I really enjoy everyone here, but it's time to move on and to be independent again. When I first arrived, several months ago, I thought most of the residents were horrible creatures and I detested them. Now I like them all; my attitudes have altered completely.

My experiences with the hippies in Brighton began the change in my personality and opened my mind. You never feel you can change at my age but lots of things have happened to me lately which I thought weren't possible. People sleeping on the beach and mixing with each other at a very deep level. They made me more aware of myself. It made me want to be more generous and give more of myself. Previously, I was a person who kept everything. With the hippies I learnt to give more easily and freely. It was a community based on give and take. Now, for the first time, I give more than I can take. I have learnt that companionship is worth much more than mere material possessions.

Thelma is dead now. A malignant cancerous growth was discovered and she was given only a few weeks to live. She was nursed by her family in the Midlands town in which she was brought up and died as a grandmother surrounded by her own large family.

7

FIONA

Fiona lived at the Lambeth Shelter for about six months. She is now nineteen, a pretty, plump and vivacious girl, but when she talks about herself her voice is laden with sadness and depression. At the time of the interviews she had been going steady with Sandy, the person in the next chapter, for about six months. This relationship, which was full of intimate and loving contact, as well as considerable horseplay, broke up several months ago.

She has now left the Shelter. She had gradually become more aggressive and petulant. Other residents expressed considerable hostility at house meetings over her refusal to play a full part in communal activities, washing up and cleaning. When she left she disappeared into the Piccadilly drug scene. She was last seen in Tottenham Court Road looking very old and physically run down. It is highly probable that she is fixing Chinese heroin.

I first left home at just fifteen, about a year and a half ago. My mother and father have been divorced for about eight years. My mother has married again and my father is living with someone else in Liverpool. I get on very badly with my stepfather and always have. My real father was in and out of prison for warehouse-breaking.

I spent the first years of my life in Glasgow, then we moved to Dumfries which is a boring little Scottish town. We stayed there until I was eight and moved to Manchester just after the marriage broke up. After the divorce we moved back to Dumfries.

I didn't see my real father for some years. I always thought there was nobody quite like him. I'm the image of him with the same looks and personality. My mother keeps telling me I'm no good really because I'm so like him. My Dad's not really the type to settle down, he ought never to have got married. He's always on the move. Dad was a good worker in between prison stretches. He took me everywhere with him. We went up to Glasgow for weekends, returning to the orphanage where he and my mother had first met.

I never saw all that much of my mother because she was working all day. There are three of us MacDonalds, Elizabeth is fourteen now and Tom is two years younger. Then there are four step-brothers, Rob is seven and David, Fergus and Stewart are all younger.

My mother lived with my stepfather for a good few years before they actually got married. He was half Scots and half French and I never liked him from the start. My father was very popular in Dumfries, but stepfather doesn't mix with anybody. He comes home from work and just sits at the table and hardly even talks to my mother. He drinks pretty heavily as well.

So at fifteen I left all this for more freedom and adventure and went to my father in Liverpool. I was frightened with my father. My mother wasn't strict, but she used to tell me what was right and wrong. My father never did. He never seemed to care about what I did and although in one way this was all right, in another it left me pretty confused. There was nobody to keep me in order and so I got really out of hand. I started working in a night club, serving behind the bar, and still my father didn't seem to care. I was staying out all night. The woman he lived with hated me. All her own children were in homes and she didn't seem to care about them, but she did care about the child she had had by my father.

She was jealous of me. She was always telling my father that she'd leave. I couldn't get over her and my father: when he lived with my mother he did what he liked, but this other woman had him wrapped around her little finger. I thought so much of him, I gave him a pound each week for spending money. But all this love was mainly on my side because he was always so wrapped up in himself. I was always trying to get closer to him.

I started to go downhill at this time. Liverpool is like the West End except that everything is run by Greek Cypriots. At first, I didn't really know what was going on. Being brought up in Scotland you're a bit thick and stupid about big cities. You're brought up with your parents, have your tea, watch television and go to bed. Until I was fourteen I wasn't allowed over the door at night.

After a while, I got sick of Liverpool and went to London. The only people I knew were Greeks. I helped out in a café, but the Greek owner got ideas about becoming a ponce. He thought I was going to be a prostitute but I wouldn't do it even if I was starving on the streets.

I started serving behind the bar in a night club and men would come in and ask me for sex. It wasn't a nice place and there were prostitutes working a pick-up service and a terrific amount of hard drinking and pot smoking. It definitely wasn't the place for a fifteen year old girl to be. Then I started on drugs. I smoked hash nearly every night in Liverpool, but never took any pills. In London, hash wasn't doing anything for me so I started on blues and bombers (Drinamyl and barbiturates). I got as thin as a rake and looked like a walking skeleton. I wasn't sleeping at night and so started skin-popping Phyceptone. This made me more ill than anything so I gave up and went back to bombers.

I was going down to the Limbo club every night and it was often raided. One night the lights started flashing and the juke-box was playing so we knew it was a police raid. I had all these bombers and blues and was stuffing them into my mouth like sweets, choking and spitting on them. A woman cop tapped me on the shoulder and said, 'Come down to the station'. I went with them completely stoned and they didn't notice, even though my eyes were as big as saucers. They questioned me and my mate and because I was stoned I told them everything, the truth about myself and what I'd been doing. They took my mate back to the approved school because she was on the run. There was a big scene where we both fought with the cops, kicked them and tried to hang on to each other until we were finally separated. They couldn't take me to a remand centre because I hadn't appeared in court, so I went to a Children's Home in Essex.

I was going to run away until I heard my mother was coming. It was really quite nice. I went swimming and helped look after the children as there was nobody of my age there. Eventually, I went before the court and got sent to Cumberlow Lodge, a remand centre. My mother was sitting in the court and she wouldn't look at me. I was smoking in the waiting room when she came in. She'd never seen me smoking before and I hid the cigarette. 'It's no good young lady, I've seen you', she said. She began to read the police statement and came to the part where it said I had lesbian tendencies. She just cried and couldn't say anything. Later she was much better and begged me to come home. I didn't know what to say.

I went to the remand centre for three weeks and it was routine. We got up at seven and after breakfast did domestic duties. I had to scrub a massive corridor on my hands and knees with a scrubbing brush and bucket. In the morning we learned to type and after dinner we'd paint and write. In the evenings we'd come home and one week we had a bath before tea and the next after tea. One of my mates came to the centre. I didn't recognize her for two days because I was always so stoned on the Dilly. She was a butch lesbian and we went everywhere together. Every week I went to see the psychiatrist and he asked me funny questions about whether I had lesbian tendencies. I said no. It got nearer to the second court appearance. My mother wrote and said things would be different if I came back. I wrote a nasty letter saying I didn't want to go back at any cost.

I didn't think my mother would come to the court after this, but she did. I was fine on the night before until bedtime. Just as I was getting my clothes together I collapsed and became hysterical and weepy. The court put me on a probation order in Dumfries back living with my mother and stepfather. I stayed there for six months until August, 1970 then returned to Liverpool to my real father. I told him it was just for a few days, but he knew better.

After a few weeks I became cheesed off. I travelled down to London and met John, who I'd met previously and lived at his flat in Aldgate. Soon after my arrival there was a burglary downstairs and the police questioned us. They found out I'd broken my probation order and wanted to fly me back. I contacted the Westminster Probation Officer, who had spoken for me in court, and she arranged for the order to be transferred to London. She found some accommodation at a Salvation Army Hostel. I hated it there. They didn't understand young girls at all. I left there after a week. Things got rather difficult so my Probation Officer found me a place at the Christian Action Shelter where I've been for about four months now.

I suppose I am what you call a lesbian. I have had sex with men, but never really enjoyed it. You have to find out what you are. It was when I first left home with a young boy in Liverpool. I just didn't like it, just didn't get anything out of it at all. One boy gave me some pleasure — that was Michaelis in Liverpool — he was nearly thirty and married. His wife was a prostitute and working for him. When he made love it was nice. We had a big fight and I broke with him because he was married and his wife was expecting. I am not a marriage breaker.

When I first came to London I got raped. I was down in the West End with two friends, both butch lesbians. We went round to several clubs: the Blue Gardenia, the Take Five and the Limbo. Later in the evening we were grabbed hold of by two big Jamaicans. My mate was thrown across the floor and Terry was knifed. She was lucky because although she was scarred it was not on her face. I was dragged upstairs into the back of the place. Then both Jamaicans carried on; one held me while the other. . . That's why I can't stand coloured people near me.

When I first came to London, I wasn't even sure what lesbians were. I met a few in Liverpool of course, but it never dawned on me that I'd ever go with a woman. I went down the West End one night and stood on the corner of Wardour Street and these two came over. They were butches and I was afraid at first. Then one night I went down to the Limbo with this fellow I was going with and he went out for a little while. This butch came over and asked for a dance. I got up and danced and packed the feller in.

I went with this girl called Terry and lived in Holloway Road for about three or four months. I've had no more sexual relationships with men, just women, although I've only lived with Terry. Terry wasn't really the type for settling down. She's a bit of a kickster, that means she kicks around with other girls all the time. When we broke up it hurt me although I did not show it much. I didn't show it was bothering me at all. I was covering up. Terry likes me now. She asked me to go back. She was much older — twenty — and more experienced. It hurt me at that time, but I've got over it now. At the time I was very depressed and went down to the Limbo and danced, but never went with anyone. Then I met this girl called Linda and was butch instead of femme, although I prefer to be femme. I went with her for about three weeks and packed her in. She went a bit mad. She was really hung up on me. I was in the Limbo one night when she walked in. I was dancing with this girl and she belted her all over the dance floor. I still didn't want to get involved, having been hurt the last time. I was terribly afraid of getting hurt again.

Jill was next. She was hung up on me before I went with Terry. She was Terry's best mate and being her best mate, I liked her, but just couldn't get attached. I can't remember clearly what happened after that except that there were lots of girls. Most of them were older, much more experienced and mostly I was femme and not butch.

Just before I came to Shelter I met Sandy. I love Sandy. She and I spend most of our time together, especially in the evenings. At first Sandy didn't like the Shelter because there was butches running all over the place. But after a while she got used to it. I do love her, but the way I am now with being so badly hurt once, there is always a doubt at the back of my mind. There's nothing you can do to stop getting hurt again. You just have to accept it when it comes but this time it would really hurt me more.

Society accepts us lesbians most of the time for what we are. They don't really accept us deep down, but most people think that it's our lives and we have got to lead them. Some men can't accept it. They shout after you in the street. If you walk up the street with a butch lesbian they can tell she isn't a man. Jamaicans especially can't stand to see a girl with another girl. If they see you with another girl they go berserk. I don't know why I'm a lesbian. Perhaps it has something to do with seeing my mother and father break up. Watching them and realizing how much it hurt me while they did it. It didn't seem to hurt them, but it really hurt me. After my father went I changed. I used to be very quiet, but I became a right devil. I wouldn't come when my mother called and although only eight, I'd stay out until midnight. I wouldn't go in and my mother would have the police out looking for me. I don't feel there's anything wrong. It hasn't been written in a law which says that a woman must go with a fellow. People have decided that for themselves. Some people have decided that they don't want to go with the opposite sex, and I'm one of them.

Sometimes I get very sad. I've made three attempts on my life. The first time was Christmas Eve last year. I was in Trafalgar Square thinking about my mother. I had a bottle of Tuinal in my pocket and I went down to the toilets and took the whole bottle. Somebody must have rung for an ambulance. I don't even know what hospital I was in. They gave me a stomach pump; I came round and walked out after a bit. I wouldn't tell them who I was or anything.

A week later on the New Year's Eve, I did the same thing. It was the first Christmas and New Year I had spent away from home. New Year hit me a bit more because every New Year my mother and I clean up the whole house, put decorations up and make hot soup. In Trafalgar Square everyone else seemed to be enjoying themselves, but to me it wasn't like New Year at all.

The next time was when Sandy and I had a big row. Sandy went down to see an old girl-friend just out of Holloway. She pretended she was going to see a man, but I knew better. When she came in and told me a lot of lies we had an enormous row. She hit me and left.

Later she told me it was finished and I said all right, even though it was hurting awfully inside. I got more and more depressed. I had been on sleepers for some time. I just kept on and on taking sleepers and yet I was still awake. Mary had taken a bottle of sleepers and there was me trying to look after her in the ambulance on the way to hospital. I went to make a phone call to tell the Christian Action Social Worker how Mary was getting on and just collapsed and was out cold for several hours. When I came round I wouldn't let them give me a stomach pump.

I am supposed to be still seeing the psychiatrist at St Thomas's. I only go when I feel like doing something stupid. I've only been twice. I don't feel as if I need psychiatric treatment. We talk about things in a general sort of way, how I'm getting on and why I left home. It doesn't do me any good and I come home none the wiser. It's a waste of his time and mine. He's just not getting through. I need to be told things about myself, I want to know why I'm so unhappy for long stretches.

I'm a very jealous and domineering person. Some people say I'm very hard on the outside. There is a soft spot in me, but it takes a little while for it to show through. I never seem to have any sympathy for anybody. When people are hurt in any way it doesn't seem to affect me. I'm very afraid of being dominated. If Sandy orders me to make a cup of tea, I won't do it. Even if she hits me I won't do it. If someone says you must do this and you mustn't do that, I can't stand it. I just get more and more stubborn. If someone tells me not to take the pills, I just go right ahead and take them. When I was little my mother used always to be saying, 'Don't do this, don't do that' and my Dad would be saying, 'Go on then, do it if you want to'.

Sometimes I cry — quite often really — but always when

alone. I cry about my family, mostly about my mother. I've hurt her in a lot of ways. I've worried her and made her older before her time. I've put her in hospital a couple of times with nervous breakdowns when I've left for London. I think a lot about the sort of person I've made myself into while I've been away from home. I regret leaving home, but I can't go back now.

I can't really be happy in a community like this one. I won't be able to live here much longer. Although I get on well with most people here, I just can't settle down properly among a group. My attitude is, that if people can't accept you the way you are they shouldn't condemn you. There is one particular person who is always telling the social workers about me. Every time I put one pill in my mouth she is down to the office like a shot. When I'm in a community I try and impress people more than anything else. They all think I'm very sympathetic, but I'm not. They don't really get through to me. One minute I'm all friendly with people and the next I can't stand anyone round me. Even when Sandy comes down and I think a terrible lot about her, sometimes I can't stand to be talked to. I think I've got a split personality. In here I think I'm one sort of person and outside another. The one outside is much worse. For so long in here, I behave myself and don't take pills. But outside in the Dilly I go back to being what I was before. When I'm here I've got people saying don't take them. Outside nobody says that. One minute I'm being like a little goodie goodie, and the next I've gone again. I'll stay in the Shelter until I find a flat. I'm going to stay off drugs for good now. I've made my decision: it's either Sandy or the drugs. Once we get a flat I'll settle down a lot better. Once Sandy and I get out of the group we'll be fine.

8

SANDY

This interview took place just over a year after the last one. Fiona and Sandy had long since broken up and we had had no contact with Fiona for several months. She was last heard of in the North London area, still on pills. Sandy had not yet 'got out of the group'.

Sandy is now nineteen. She is short and stocky with short hair and usually dresses in men's clothing. She is one of the main 'characters' at Greek Street. She first had contact with the old Lambeth Shelter when she was about fourteen. She and her brother Sam were frequent visitors as they fled from their shouting, screaming, drunken mother.

Some years later she moved in to the Shelter as a resident after a stormy row with mother. She is well liked by both the staff and residents for her cockney lip and humour. Occasionally she gets fighting drunk and has noisy arguments with staff members. Several months ago she started threatening and bullying an older resident, and was asked to leave Greek Street for a month. She was allowed to return and has been there ever since.

Although Sandy lives in a large project for homeless women, she is certainly not homeless in the traditional sense. She has a 'home' in Lambeth to which she could certainly return. She has a reasonable, well-paid job and could probably find private accommodation in central London. Then why does she stay at Greek Street? In many ways, Sandy has never known what it is like to have a real home and Greek Street is the nearest equivalent to it.

I was born nineteen years ago in Hammersmith, London.

I have a brother Ian, two years older and Sam who is only thirteen. Well, Sam isn't my real brother. You see his father was different from mine. I don't know who he was.

I don't like Ian. He's mentally retarded and always thinks he's right. You can't tell him anything. He still lives with my mother because he's too stupid to get married. He works on and off on the building sites and lives in a childish world of Germans. There are helmets and bayonets all over his bedroom wall. He would like to have been German because he says they won the last war. Young Sam goes to a special school which helps him to read and write. He didn't use to go to school very often so he's got behind all the others in his class.

I didn't know my father really. He worked in a bank the last I heard of him. I've met him a few times but he got divorced from my mother when I was very small. My mother is all right when she's not drunk, but then. . . she's murder. She slags you and goes mad. She used to bring blokes home and I'd cheek them when I was smaller and tell them to go. She'd attack me and call me names like, 'You dirty bastard, you're no use to me', and, 'You're not my real daughter'. She was drunk you see and didn't know what she was doing and then she'd hit me with a Guinness bottle.

When I was really little I didn't see much of her. When I was about two years old she got evicted and had to go into Homeless Families Accommodation and I went into a Council Home in Surrey. I was completely on my own. The names of the houses were trees and I lived in Beech House. It was bloody horrible. They punished you all the time. They used to stop your pocket money and once I had to stand in the kitchen all night long. I'd wet the bed or something and they just forgot about me. I used to wet the bed until I was about thirteen. I still do

occasionally when I'm very drunk. The Children's Home
sent me to the Child Guidance clinic for it. I had to go
once a week to a hospital and play with the sand and toys.

On the whole I got on well with both the staff and
the kids in the home. There were lots of us. For a year
or two I was shifted to a smaller home with only seven
kids in Langley, Bucks. It was more homely. The staff
in charge had more time and could give us more attention. But then they shifted me back to Surrey again. I
was very fond of the staff. They were all women. I enjoyed going shopping with them and holding the large
bag full of groceries. The Home also had a school. It was
like a village really, there was hardly any need to go out.
It reminds me of Greek Street. I got on well at the
school, although I was neither very good or very bad. I
can write fairly well apart from the spelling, but reading
is sometimes difficult. I have a problem making out some
of the words. I used to do a lot of games, climb trees
and play football with the boys.

At ten I left the Children's Home and went back to
live with my mother and two brothers in a council flat
in Millbank. I got on quite well with her even though
that was the time when she started belting me. It was a
rough old life because she never had any bloody money.
She was living off social security and drinking most of it.
We just went without. She was always behind with the
rent and often there was no food in the cupboard when
we came home from school and we just had to wait for
the free school dinners the following day. You soon got
used to it. She would go without food herself to give it
to us kids, but she just didn't have it because of her
liking for the booze. You see it was an obsession with
her. She couldn't help it. She drinks Guinness all the
time. Men bring her home dead drunk from the pub and
think they're going to bed with her.

Leaving the Children's Home meant a change of school as well. I really enjoyed my last years at school. I mixed well with other kids because I'm so outgoing and generally cheerful and I had lots of friends. I was in the school sports playing netball. By that time we'd moved over the river to Lambeth, quite near the old Christian Action shelter.

At fifteen I left school and went to work in an Art agency as a general office girl. I was there for eighteen months and really liked it. I left to work in the Royal Free Hospital laundry because it was much more money. It was very hot and hard, but I got fifteen pounds a week instead of only six.

My mates used to live next door to 12 Lambeth High Street (the old Lambeth Shelter) which had been empty. One day we kept seeing people go in and out and then we learnt it was going to be used as a hostel for homeless women. We offered to help with the painting and then it opened and I used to go around quite a lot in the evenings. That was over six years ago. I really wanted to go and live there. It had such a friendly atmosphere despite all the fights and disturbances. I made great friends with the Christian Action social worker and knew most of the residents. It was there I first met Fiona and Rosie (her present girl-friend). I was very fond of the old Shelter and sad when it was moved to Greek Street.

It never occurred to me that I would leave my mother until two or three years back. The crunch came one night when she came home from the pub very drunk with a couple of blokes holding her up. We had a huge row and she hit me with a beer bottle and I decided I just wasn't taking any more and left. I walked round to Christian Action and moved into Lambeth High Street. Then I went back to Mum taking Rosie with me, but it didn't last. After another blazing row we came to stay at Greek

Street roughly seven or eight months ago. Although I still keep contact with my mother, I don't think I'll go back to live there again. It just doesn't work out.

I've never been much interested in boys. They're fine for playing football with, but not for sex. When I was at school I used to fancy the women teachers, but I thought that was only a phase that most girls go through. I didn't let it worry me. But later, as I got older, I still fancied the girls and I wanted to sleep with them and not the boys. I just fell for girls more that's all. Rosie was the first girl I went with. I've had quite a few since her. She gets very jealous and possessive. If I went out to the pictures with a girl she would let me know that I had done something wrong by humiliating me, shouting at me, show me up in front of people, generally treat me as if I was a bit of a kid. We've been very close for over five years. I even went to stay at her home in Ireland. Her family lived right out in the country. I liked it for a few days and then it was just very boring. There was nothing to do. At Easter this year Rosie went back to Ireland by herself. She slept with this fellow and got herself pregnant. She came back to London and told me and I wasn't angry or anything. I didn't mind. She's expecting the kid in late December just near my birthday. I keep in touch with her by letter and over the phone. She ought to settle down and take care of a family. She is a very shy person, fond of housework and keeping things tidy. She's not really for me, although we did everything together for so many years. I don't miss her much at the moment, but then she's only been gone about two weeks. I practically forced her to go back home to Ireland by being so nasty. I went about with different birds and I knew the jealousy would kill her and she'd go back home. Finally, she couldn't take any more. She brings out all the nastiness and violence in me. She makes me feel claustrophobic, or whatever you call it.

I don't have much trouble in attracting the birds. You don't if you're good-looking like me. Being a lesbian doesn't make life difficult. I still get on well with the blokes. I like a fellow's company, but I couldn't go to bed with one. I'm butch in my dress and in my outlook, but I'm still female inside. I know I'm a girl. I love kids and would like to adopt one. I don't think I ever loved Rosie, although she was a beautiful girl. I love my mother and wouldn't change her for anyone else. When she's not full of drink she's really nice. She treats me like a daughter when sober, but when she's drunk I become a nobody. She likes my opinions on things. She makes me feel as if she really needs me.

I don't waste much time thinking or worrying about things. I'm too busy living. I'd like some day to have a nice flat, someone nice to live with and an interesting job, but generally I prefer not to think much or plan the future. I know I'll never lack for work or money. I get plenty of money from my present job serving teas in a canteen. I send Rosie money, buy presents, clothes, pop records, drink and give money to some hard-up friends in Greek Street and so, in the end, land up with nothing.

Greek Street is a really terrible place to live in nowadays. There's nothing much wrong with the staff. The majority of them are fine. It's the building and some of the residents. It's filthy here nowadays. Some residents just will not wash. Their hair is infested with fleas and nits. The rooms are never swept out. A lot of people feel upset by it, but they will not speak out to the staff. They just moan to me. They think that I'll act as a general spokesman. I can't understand why people can't just be told to clean out their room or have a bath. The place is simply diabolical. There are syringe needles full of blood, and dirty clothes lying about, and a general atmosphere of drugs here. I started using them myself about a year ago. I thought, well it's doing things for my mates, why don't I have a go. I used some Tuinal and Phyceptone, which I got off some residents here. I liked it. It made me float off right up in the air. When you came down again it was like staggering around being drunk. I didn't try drugs again. I'll stick to alcohol.

I don't think I'd change much in my life looking back. Nothing much has really happened to me. I'd like to have had a real father and not to have gone into a home, but I don't really regret that. It's left me with problems. If I get attached to someone I get scared they're going to leave me. I'm frightened of being ditched. I often get very annoyed with people I care a lot about.

I'm going to be all right in my life. You see I'm toughened up because of my childhood. When I was a kid I used to take the piss out of tramps and cripples, yell insults at them and that. I wouldn't do that now, I have more sympathy. I know now how life is for them with having been through it. Most people are nice.

David, I liked you from the beginning. Rosie was always very fond of you. You were a fellow I could really talk to, but then everything changes at Greek Street. I suppose I've been jealous of you for many months. I was jealous of your relationship with the women staff. You used to be always laughing and joking with them in the staff room. I used to hate you sometimes. I thought you also took it out on me. You were often sarcastic and bad-tempered. But I don't hate you any more. I've changed again. Greek Street has had an effect on me. I'm a lot more bitchy and less patient. Before I came here I hated to see anyone suffer, but now I haven't time for people. I can't be bothered. Greek Street knocks the stuffing out of you. It's still my home despite all that.

I'd much rather be here than anywhere else. It was terrible when I got banned for a month for bullying an older resident. When you've never really had a home like me, this place gives you a sort of deep security. I am well aware that almost all the people who sincerely care about me in the entire world live or work here in this building. If I died they would genuinely miss me.

GENERAL ANALYSIS

Homelessness is an elusive and amorphous concept which tends to expose our extensive ignorance of social events and processes. For some it is a deep and lifelong experience; for others a trivial and night-long event. We ask questions, both as researchers and interested human beings, which have little relevance to those who sleep out and live from hand to mouth. We can very easily fall into the 'them and us' attitude, the trap of seeing 'us' (whoever we may be) sharing a number of common characteristics and features and those who are homeless as similarly homogeneous and, of course, different from us. It is clear that the six women whose stories we have just heard are very different from each other and come from diverse backgrounds. They have their own individuality and uniqueness.

Many of us feel guilty, attacked and even undermined by those who are homeless. We feel that it ought not to be happening; that in a civilized country whose citizens live in comparative affluence people ought not to be living in such conditions. But our approach contains a central ambivalence. We are revolted and repulsed by men pissing in bus shelters; perplexed, bewildered or just plain envious of those who seem to live comparatively free of social obligations. We have romantic fantasies of weather-beaten, string-belted tramps wandering the clean, fresh countryside, free of mortgages, nagging boss and ulcers, and free of family responsibilities. We forget the tuberculosis, the frost-bitten toes and the omnipresent lice. We forget the way in which people without homes are pushed around, preached at and spend most of their time waiting for things to happen.

Homelessness ties us in knots like a Chinese puzzle. The more we grapple with it, the more tightly we bind ourselves in it. The struggle becomes like two well-greased and superbly matched wrestlers fighting from morn to sunset, neither gaining a deciding hold. It is a dilemma and paradox very familiar to Zen Buddhism and Chinese Taoism. There is very considerable truth in the assertion that we are ourselves the problem rather than homelessness and homeless people.

That is not to say that nothing can or should be done about people sleeping rough on the Embankment or living overcrowded in stuffy and lousy lodging houses. We are desperately short of housing in the places where it is most needed and demanded and no riddle can wish that fact away. But the issue lies not only in the lack of housing and its inegalitarian distribution but in our own patronizing attitudes, the sentimental cheque-book love and the greed for possessions and property. There is a very real way in which, if there is a problem at all, it lies directly in the loving hearts of social workers who focus exclusively on individuals in distress rather than on ways to change major social injustices. We are ourselves part of the knot which we seek so desperately to unravel.[1] To undo the knot completely might mean our being less comfortable and well-housed and some damage to our own interests.

Once we begin to see people primarily as 'social problems', and it is often hard to do otherwise, we have effectively and subtly dehumanized them. Labelling planes them down efficiently into simple geometrical shapes which can be stored in intellectual cupboards: drug addicts, alcoholics, epileptics. . . . We have squeezed out the human untidiness, the uniqueness, the individuality and dignity in an attempt to be 'of help'. I remain profoundly sceptical of organized attempts to do good to others through deliberate intent. The world needs protecting against most who pursue those particular goals. It steers close to what R.D. Laing and others call the 'tyranny of love'. It murmurs softly 'I am doing this for your own good. I will love you but only after you make certain changes in the way you behave to me and the world.' It does not even allow the victim the room to get angry at the manipulations. It is the very breath of the eternal Jewish Mother in *Portnoy's Complaint*.

Such labelling provides us with an emotional shield and offers some protection against major challenges to our way of life and values. Someone who is a problem can have nothing much to add or give to our own lives. I can, in those circumstances, simply dismiss what Jean, Rosemary, Fiona and the others have to offer.

Homelessness is the last desperate refuge of the social work evangelist and romantic. He has seen his traditional areas of concern gobbled up by the professionalized social services. The twentieth century has seen a process of increasing state intervention in the field of human suffering, with local and central government doing more and more. In the field of homeless single people, voluntary societies have remained predominant, particularly such evangelical Christian groups as the Church Army and the Salvation Army. Their prevailing tendency is to look exclusively at the individuals themselves, concentrating on ambulance and crisis work and failing to provide any, except the most simplistic, analysis of how people come to be homeless in the first place.

This narrowness of perspective makes it difficult for most people to see that homelessness is frequently the result of very broad social changes and covers a much wider canvas than Skid Row and the vagrant alcoholic. Society finds it very difficult to remember that there are large numbers of homeless people stacked away in various human warehouses such as psychiatric hospitals and prisons.

This perspective also focuses exclusively on the homeless individual. It implies that his difficulties are entirely his own responsibility and can be remedied completely by extra effort and application. It sounds suspiciously like the old Protestant Ethic. However, individuals are, either in a central or peripheral way, subject to certain social pressures and changes.

A rapidly developing society requires certain forms of mobile, cheap labour. It needs large numbers of unskilled men and women at certain periods of its evolution, as for instance did Britain during the development of the railway and canal systems. We needed the gangs of Irish navvies who dug out the tunnels and canal beds and later the roads. Chains of lodging houses sprang up to house this lusty, drunken, mobile band of workers. Society provided those workers with cheap communal living accommodation and when the roads, canals and railways were built, simply discarded those who were unable to re-adapt.[2] The non-adaptors spend most of their lives unemployed or engaged in very poorly-paid work, living in poor quality accommodation.

Many homeless women fall into this category. They are bound up in three big knots. These are the intertwining ropes of therapy, employment and perhaps, most importantly, accommodation. Major changes in those three systems have far-reaching consequences for the women in derelict buildings or lodging-houses. I am not suggesting that they have no free will or are forced into a homeless way of life through no choice of their own.

One of the most basic and difficult social problems is coping with people who confuse and frighten the rest of us. What do we do with people like Peggy with her disturbing violent behaviour? I have never seen that side of her personality but I can imagine that she could have been very frightening and powerful. At present we provide a series of institutions such as psychiatric hospitals and prisons with which no one is happy. These institutions manage people extremely well but the increasing evidence is that they also inflict damage. Peggy herself realized that through her prison and mental hospital experiences she had become institutionalized and could not manage by herself. She considered the repeated use of electroconvulsive therapy a punishment for her violent behaviour. She told me that the nurses were afraid of her muscles and quick temper, and that the only way they could hit back at her was through the shock treatment.

Now she is dead. She reserved most of her violent behaviour for herself. Nowadays we are wiser and more restrained about electro-convulsive therapy. We know more about the insidious tendencies of institutional neurosis: how a person's own independence can be eroded by too long a stay in closed and protected environments. Nowadays there is a very definite attempt, albeit very slow to run down the big psychiatric hospitals and provide effective care in the community.

This trend was begun by the Mental Health Act of 1959. In the field of homelessness this Act, or more particularly the local authorities' failure to provide community care facilities, was quickly cast as the villain of the piece. Henry Rollin wrote

> since the 1959 Act, the mentally disordered have added to the problem of criminality. The sum total in terms of increased social pathology must be considerable. If the present discharge policy from mental hospitals is not matched by an increase in the facilities for community care, then there is a grave danger that the tolerance of society for the mentally disordered

in their midst will be overstrained and the future of the vastly important 1959 Act thereby imperilled.[3]

A recent National Association for Mental Health analysis of 123 local authorities' provisions for the mentally ill discovered that seventy-five had one or more hostel and forty-five authorities had no residential provision at all.[4-5] Thirteen years after the passing of the Act that is a dreadful state of affairs. Community facilities for the mentally ill and handicapped, such as day centres and hostels, need much higher priority. At present, railway stations, reception centres and night refuges form an important, if unintended, part of the total community care network.

As well as expanding the quantity of provision we need also to do something about the abysmally poor quality and narrow range of existing facilities. They tend to compete for the small proportion of 'highly motivated' residents and exclude those who are thought to be 'difficult'. Powerful ideas are voiced, but little of the heady mixture of encounter groups, re-evaluation therapy and the opportunity for residents to make important decisions, finds its way through the doors of hostels for homeless women.[6] Why not? Mainly because residential care is essentially extremely conservative and resistant to new ideas. The staff are overworked, ill-trained and poorly paid.

Greek Street, despite all its failings, has shown that working in hostels can be both challenging and exciting. It has been able to attract high quality staff. Most have had social work training, although sometimes that has been a positive handicap in the development of that openness and awareness which is so important a part of the community. The major problem has been how to cope with large numbers of women who have been badly damaged by their childhood, prison and mental hospital experiences; how to enable them to develop their un-doubted strengths and use them within the community. However, Greek Street should be an alternative to psychiatric in-patient care and imprisonment rather than a supplement.

In our society, the ability to work is closely linked with the capacity to pay for food and accommodation as well as with feelings of status and well-being. Most homeless people spend long periods unemployed. Por-tions of their week are spent queueing for unemployment, sickness, and social security pay; answering questions and filling in forms about their background, present situation and finances.

When homeless people work, they are employed in four main industries: catering, holiday trades, building and markets.[7] These are all industries which require a lot of unskilled labour, often on an irregular basis. Our six women, apart from Rosemary, usually worked as waitresses, canteen hands and cinema usherettes. Mostly they disliked their work intensely and had long stretches of unemployment. Over two thirds of all the residents of Greek Street are unemployed at any one time.

All these industries are undergoing major technolo-gical changes in an attempt to cut down labour costs. I met a man in Birmingham, living under a railway arch, who had been made unemployed, possibly permanently, simply by the installation of a washing-up machine in the café where he had worked for five years. In the build-ing industry, there has been an attempt to introduce industrialized building units to cut down labour costs and use men more efficiently. In the centre of most of our large cities, London, Birmingham and Glasgow, the markets are being re-developed. When Nine Elms replaces Covent Garden in a year or two, its mechanized processes will cut down the use of much of the casual labour hitherto employed.

In the United States, Rooney showed that the proportion of all workers engaged in unskilled non-farm labour dropped from 12.5% in 1900 to 9.4% in 1940 and to only 4.8% in 1960.[8] A major factor in employment trends in this country has been the decasualization policies agreed between the Trade Unions and management which have reduced the amount of irregular work available.

The accommodation situation has changed even more rapidly. As the Milner Holland report said

> the supply of rented accommodation in Greater London has diminished and is still diminishing fast. This trend will not be halted, still less reversed, unless investors can be assured that, providing that their properties are properly maintained and managed they will be free from the hazards of political uncertainty and able to obtain an economic return.[9]

One might well add that there are much richer pickings to be had from razing rented properties to the ground and developing them as heavily government-subsidized hotel schemes or office blocks. Centrepoint, the thirty-five storey office and flat block, in the centre of London, has become a symbol of the economic ills of the housing market. Empty since it was built in 1964, it pays its developers, Oldham Estate Company Ltd., to keep it so.

Whatever the aetiological explanation, the trend of a substantial reduction in rented accommodation is both undeniable and undesirable. In 1914, 90% of homes were rented from private landlords. By 1950 this had fallen to 44%, by 1960 to 26% and by 1971 to 14%.[10] There seems no likelihood of a reversal of this trend. In addition, cheap communal accommodation such as lodging houses, has been decreasing without any replacement. We are rapidly entering an age when the choice is between council housing, which necessarily gives priority

to families, and the 'property owning democracy'.
Successive pieces of legislation, particularly the most
recent Housing Finance Act (1972), actually aggravate
the situation by placing, in certain circumstances, dis-
incentives to taking in lodgers.[11]

This situation is not confined to England. The redevelopment of central urban areas, within reach of
transport systems and rail termini and with high site
values, is a major feature of contemporary France, Western
Germany and Italy. In Glasgow, families have been
moved out of the poor housing of the Gorbals, close
to the city centre, eight miles away to Easterhouse and
other vast housing estates. The valuable sites of lodging-houses, built mostly over fifty years ago, are
sold and redeveloped and the beds for homeless single
people lost, probably for ever. For example, it would
take all the Glasgow voluntary societies over thirty
years of activity, at their present rate of expansion,
merely to replace the 1,275 beds in lodging houses
which have been lost in the last decade. This makes
their preoccupation with running small shelters and
day centres rather than an involvement with wider
political activity even sadder.

The trend of a massive reduction in the rented
accommodation sector is extremely important. It is
this side of the housing market which has traditionally
housed so many of the elderly, the physically handicapped and the mentally ill.[12] These are the very
people who find it most difficult to compete on the
open housing market. They cannot work for long periods
of time. They cannot find highly paid employment because they lack education and skills. Many people are
finding, and will increasingly find themselves squeezed
down and, in some cases, out of the market altogether.[13]

More specifically, what problems do homeless women

present and what, if anything, can or needs to be done?

There are certainly changes and phenomena about which precious little can be done. One consequence of the increased emancipation of women is an increase in the number sleeping rough and living in poor quality accommodation away from their homes. If society presents women with (or they take) a greater variety of life styles or social choices, some will decide to leave home, family and neighbourhood and in a situation where there is a serious shortage of accommodation a small number of these will eventually become homeless.

These women are exposed to all sorts of social problems and stresses. They may find it very difficult to get money and work. They are no longer part of the nuclear or extended family systems. They must make their own way; make their own set of relationships, usually among men and women in similar circumstances.

Many of these women are Irish or Scots in origin. Some are attempting to find a new life for themselves away from the troubles of their own home town. They may stay a few days in London, find it too rough and tough and return home to their families. In the large cities, short stay accommodation especially becomes very difficult to find and so these women increasingly find themselves stranded in the night shelters and hostels of the voluntary societies. Many of these services regard their users as having 'serious problems'.

There is a pressing need to develop new systems of housing like the nineteenth century lodging houses for single people. We need many different sorts of provision: some women are able to live independent existences with no outside help; others need occasional assistance and others again require fairly extensive care and guidance. It should be possible to develop sites in or near our large cities to provide a diversity of services. The Department of the Environment is experimenting with different building designs for accommodating single people.[14]

In the short term, we need to halt the impending closure of lodging houses until we have worked out an effective replacement policy. The government report on lodging houses and hostels shows that during the period October 1965 to October 1972 we lost about 17% of the total available beds.[15] This is a very serious situation and we cannot allow it to continue. Local authorities are naturally anxious to redevelop the older and decayed areas such as Hays Wharf in Southwark where there are a number of cheap hostels and lodging houses. It brings them in extra rate revenue. If they are not to do so, they will probably need to be compensated. Present government financial aid for the building of large hostels is grossly inadequate.

Particular London boroughs shoulder much more than their fair share of the whole problem. The London Borough of Lewisham recently began a campaign to expand the number of lodgings available within the borough. Croydon and Edinburgh have both experimented with lodgings schemes for the mentally ill. 'After Six', a newly formed voluntary organization, provides a splendid service advising thousands of homeless people on the availability of rented accommodation by pinpointing vacancies in rented rooms in various parts of London.[16] In addition to these schemes there is a strong case for rate rebates or income concessions to those who take in strangers as lodgers. This would be one way of encouraging a more efficient use of under-occupied housing.

One major block to effective policies for homelessness is the widespread administrative confusion which has bedevilled local and central government for centuries. How can groups of people who refuse to play the game according to the agreed rules be dealt with? Long before the settlement acts of the fourteenth century, those who made the laws and lived in homes have tried to cajole, compel and more recently to entice the homeless to behave in, what we see as, a more reasonable manner. Such efforts have mostly failed.

There is a story about an Irishman who, when asked where Trafalgar Square was said, 'Well, if I was going there, I wouldn't be starting from here'. That Irishman is probably a senior civil servant in the Department of Health and Social Security. The whole foundation of government policy is that homeless people must be changed in some way. Some years ago I remember having a furious row with a Cabinet Minister who told me he was going to transfer all the hundreds of homeless mentally ill people from the reception centres to the network of two hundred after-care hostels which were shortly to be developed. The whole exercise was to be as smooth as a military manoeuvre. I tried to explain to him, in vain, that there was just one snag: the men were not conscripts and that most of them simply would not go to the new units.

The Department of Health has responsibility for accommodation within the terms of the 1948 National Assistance Act. Within the Department, the Supplementary Benefits Commission (S.B.C.) has a duty to see that 'temporary accommodation for persons without a settled way of living' is provided where appropriate. Most reception centres are administered directly by the S.B.C. although there are still a few for which the local authorities are managing agents.

Another wing of the Department of Health attempts, largely unsuccessfully, to persuade local authorities to provide residential care for the mentally ill and handicapped and to interpret the National Assistance Acts phrase 'for those in need of care and attention' in a wider sense.[17] Local authorities have a broad, and frequently vague, responsibility to provide longer term accommodation for a variety of socio-medical situations. At present, they are mostly floundering in the enlarged responsibilities which the 1970 Social Services Act has placed upon them. My own view is that although social service departments must eventually take over responsibility for single homelessness in most of its aspects, at present they are unwilling and unable to do so. With a largely static population of homeless people, the old argument that the high mobility of the problem requires national administration no longer holds.

As if all this were not sufficiently complex, the Home Office and the Department of the Environment enter, like Laurel and Hardy from the wings. The Home Office has responsibility for over-seeing the development and funding of residential facilities for homeless offenders and much of the fostering of hostels is done by the government-sponsored Bridgehead Housing Association. The Department of Environment looks at twilight zones of large cities and is concerned particularly with the lodging house problem.

In such a complicated situation it is frequently difficult to discover who is responsible for a particular problem, which seems to be everyone's and no one's at the same time. We require an overall strategy for homelessness which uses the combined resources of voluntary and statutory bodies in the most relevant and efficacious way. Statutory bodies have more resources — buildings, trained manpower, finance — whereas voluntary organizations have the advantage of much speedier reactions and far greater flexibility. We are moving steadily towards the development of reception centres as places for assessment and diagnosis with a concentration of workshops, retraining, medical and psychiatric facilities which no voluntary body can afford. The reception centres presently lack the trained staff and expertise to provide effective social work.

Voluntary societies need to concentrate on contact and experimental projects. Soup runs, night shelters, peripatetic street contact work, are all areas which require infinite flexibility as shown by the Archway Project and the Simon Community.[18-19] Although voluntary societies must inevitably retain some sort of role in the field of long term care, local authorities will have to be encouraged, and frequently coerced and driven to play a more extensive part. The residential side of the Welfare State has been very slow to develop in comparison with the field-work element. All the social workers in the world will not keep the rain off one homeless man's back.

In the past, there has been a marked tendency for local authorities to see voluntary activity as a substitute for their own action rather than a supplement to it. In Christian Action we had to avoid being used in this way on a number of occasions. The Butterwick House affair was one specific example. Butterwick was one of the Rowton Houses with 750 beds which closed down in the summer of 1972 as a result of the London Borough of Hammersmith's redevelopment plans. It used the activities of two small voluntary societies, the St Mungos Community and the Cyrenians, to establish seven hostels for just over one hundred men in houses provided by the London Borough, as a smokescreen for doing virtually nothing itself.

Voluntary societies have long been dominated by nineteenth century attitudes. They have preferred slogans and glossy manifestos to honest questions and research. I feel that the Salvation Army, in particular, has a lot to answer for in stacking thousands of homeless men away in its hostels and doing very little real social work or human relations. But the Army is not alone; the whole emphasis has been on ambulance rather than preventive work; on meeting the current situation rather than on trying to find out why it happens at all.

Too often, as in Glasgow, small voluntary bodies concentrate all their energies on the caring work and do not see impending social avalanches. There, several dozen voluntary societies struggle to provide soup runs, day centres and night shelters to a few hundred men while all around them hundreds of beds for single people disappear, through housing and redevelopment programmes, without a protest being raised.[20] I suppose it is another example of how much more exciting it is to save one life through a heart transplant rather than a hundred through better sanitation.

In Britain, voluntary societies in this field are small, fragmented and parochial. Traditionally, they are the concrete manifestations of the empire-building aspirations of a few dynamic people. They run one or two projects and cultivate their own little cabbage patch in Aberdeen or Scunthorpe, with little regard for anything happening elsewhere. Of course there are regional and local differences in patterns of homelessness and it is right that these should be met by voluntary bodies who are sensitive to those different needs. The tragedy is that the fragmentation of those bodies means that homelessness has little political musclepower and that even the most sincere and sensitive of Ministers is deafened by a Tower of Babel when he listens for advice. These tiny, parochial organizations, true English amateurs, are competing increasingly against well-organized voluntary bodies such as Shelter, the National Association for Mental Health and the Spastics Society for a larger slice of the same cake. They have a pressing need to become more professional, to operate nationally and

to be more politically aggressive. The government-finan-
ced Campaign for the Homeless and Rootless, to which
a large number of bodies have already affiliated, might
provide the necessary focus.

Despite these difficulties, it is essential to be optimistic about the long-term future of homelessness. The
problem is a grave one and it may well get rather worse
over the next four or five years. However, there are
signs that society seeks to formulate sensible, sensitive
and relevant questions rather than provide a barrage of
shallow answers. David Tidmarsh's research at Camberwell reception centre and the large government grant to
St Mungos Community for research into homeless alcoholics are indications of this genuine quest for knowledge
and more enlightened policies.[21]

In the field of government reports and legislation,
both the 'Habitual Drunkenness Offender' report and
the Criminal Justice Act, 1969, with their emphasis on
moving the sick away from punishment to care and
attention are worthy of the twentieth century.[22] Overall
there is a greater mood of co-operation between statutory
and voluntary bodies. There is an increased number of
joint schemes, with voluntary societies providing flexibility and enthusiasm and central government giving money
and other resources.

Nowadays, I have a vested interest in being optimistic.
To be pessimistic would be to undermine and devalue
the most important part of my last ten years' work. The
angry young social worker I used to be is now a welcome
figure at Alexander Fleming House, the headquarters of
the Department of Health and Social Security. I am the
current holder of a government research grant into
juvenile homelessness and have become a part of the
whole establishment process.

Those experiences which have been the most worthwhile have not been research or administrative ones. They have been the deep and lasting contact with both social workers and homeless people. I have been taught to be more open, aware and loving. I only wish I were more so.

If we are to arrive at a greater understanding of homelessness, for there can be no ultimate solution, it cannot be by merely providing a more efficient administrative structure. 'Doing something' about homelessness must mean caring more about one another; questioning closely our beliefs in the sacredness of property. The six homeless women in this book are neither 'monsters' nor objects for our pity or compassion. What has happened to them cannot be undone. We have much to learn from their various strengths and they offer us a different conception and perspective on life. It is a shifting, wandering existence cut off from most traditional social responsibilities: husbands and children. How far we are prepared to truly understand that perspective and let it challenge our own is also the extent to which real progress in homelessness can be achieved.

REFERENCES

1 Alan Watts, *Psychotherapy East and West.* Peter Owen 1971.

2 David Brandon, *The Treadmill.* Christian Action 1969.

3 Henry Rollin, 'From Patients into Vagrants' (*New Society,* 15 January 1970).

4 *Community Care Provision for the Mentally Ill.* National Association for Mental Health, October 1971.

5 Elizabeth Durkin, *Hostels for the Mentally Disordered.* Young Fabian Pamphlet 24, 1971.

6 Dennie Briggs, Stuart Whiteley, Merfyn Turner, *Dealing with Deviants.* Hogarth Press 1972.

7 National Assistance Board, *Homeless Single Persons.* H.M.S.O. 1966.

8   Howard Bahr, ed., *Disaffiliated Man.* University of Toronto Press 1970.
9   *Report of the Committee on Housing in Greater London.* Cmd 2605, H.M.S.O. 1965.
10 Anthony Crossland, 'The Tenants Hopeful Estate' (*The Guardian*, 16 June 1972).
11 *Poverty* No. 22 (Spring 1972) Child Poverty Action Group.
12 David Donnison, 'No More Reports' (*New Society*, 27 May 1971).
13 David Brandon, *Homeless in London.* Christian Action 1971 (revised 1973).
14 Department of the Environment, *Housing Single People (1).* H.M.S.O. 1971.
15 'Accommodation for the Homeless Young' (*Hansard* House of Lords, 16 April 1973, 341: No. 71) H.M.S.O.
16 Peter Beresford, 'After Six' (*Social Work Today*, March 1974).
17 *Homeless Single Persons in Need of Care and Support.* Department of Health and Social Security circular 37/72, September 1972.
18 *Report — Volumes I, II and III.* Brighton Archways Venture 1971.
19 *Yesterday's Youth. . .Today's Tragedy.* Simon Community Report 406, 1970.
20 Dione Croussaz, *Glasgow's Homeless Single People*. Christian Action 1972.
21 David Tidmarsh, Susanne Wood, 'The Psychiatric Aspects of Destitution' in J.K. Wing, ed., *An Evaluation of a Community Psychiatric Service*, Oxford University Press 1972.
22 Home Office, *Habitual Drunkenness Offenders*. H.M.S.O. 1971.